FRESH INDIAN

SUNIL VIJAYAKAR

hamlyn

IN MEMORY OF LEON

First published in Great Britain in 2007 by
Hamlyn, a division of Octopus Publishing Group Ltd
2–4 Heron Quays, London E14 4JP

Copyright © Octopus Publishing Group Ltd 2007

The material in this book was previously published in
Fresh Indian

ISBN-13: 978-0-600-61686-3
ISBN-10: 0-600-61686-X

A CIP catalogue record for this book is available
from the British Library

Printed and bound in China

10 9 8 7 6 5 4 3 2 1

NOTE

Both metric and imperial measurements have been given in all
recipes. Use one set of measurements only and not a mixture
of both.

Standard level spoon measurements are used in all recipes.
1 tablespoon – one 15 ml spoon
1 teaspoon = one 5 ml spoon

The Department of Health advises that eggs should not be
consumed raw. This book contains dishes made with raw or
lightly cooked eggs. It is prudent for vulnerable people such as
pregnant and nursing mothers, invalids, the elderly, babies and
young children to avoid uncooked or lightly cooked dishes
made with eggs. Once prepared, these dishes should be kept
refrigerated and used promptly.

This book includes dishes made with nuts and nut derivatives.
It is advisable for those with known allergic reactions to nuts
and nut derivatives and those who may be potentially
vulnerable to these allergies, such as pregnant and nursing
mothers, invalids, the elderly, babies and children to avoid
dishes made with nuts and nut oils. It is also prudent to check
the labels of pre-prepared ingredients for the possible inclusion
of nut derivatives.

Ovens should be preheated to the specified temperature – if
using a fan-assisted oven, follow the manufacturer's
instructions for adjusting the time and the temperature.

CONTENTS

INTRODUCTION

For many, the idea of Indian food is one of high-fat, high-calorie dishes cooked in saturated fat and swimming with oil. But the truth is, Indian cuisine can be light and healthy, with fresh flavours, fabulous colours and delicious textures. This book offers a modern approach to traditional Indian cooking, creating classic flavours and dishes using nutritious, low-fat ingredients and making use of healthy cooking techniques to achieve perfect, guilt-free and authentic results.

There's a wide choice of both hot and mild dishes, some with light, fresh flavours, others with the mouth-watering, comforting texture of a slow-simmered dhal. The recipes have been designed with the modern cook in mind – making use of healthy ingredients that are fresh, delicious and bursting with flavour.

A well-stocked pantry of basic ingredients and spices is essential. Most of these can be bought in large super-markets, but I would urge you to visit an Indian or Asian market and stock up with a range of ingredients. Don't let yourself be intimidated by ingredients that may be new to you. Just make sure that you have everything laid out and on hand before you start to cook, and the rest will be easy.

At the end of the day, the main ingredient to have at hand is the love, enjoyment and passion for food, cooking and eating. Don't be afraid to experiment so that you can understand the cooking techniques you employ, the ingredients you use and the flavours and textures you create. As long as you approach your time in the kitchen in a relaxed, calm and confident manner, following your own instincts and trusting your own palette, you can be confident of forging ahead to a delicious, healthy and flavourful way of life to share with family and friends.

SUNIL VIJAYAKAR

FRESH AND HEALTHY

The recipes in this book have all been devised with healthy eating in mind, using the healthiest ingredients and cooking techniques possible. They concentrate on cutting down on fat and salt and using fresh, wholesome ingredients to provide you with the fuel you need to stay healthy and fit. Many dishes, such as the chutneys and salads, use raw fruit and vegetables, while others lightly cook them, tossing them with spices until they are just tender and still retain all their valuable nutrients. Low-fat cuts of meat and poultry are used in the recipes, and there are plenty of dishes containing healthy oily fish, which contain the essential fatty acids that are so important for good health.

Fat is the real villain in traditional Indian cooking, with most recipes starting with frying spices in ghee (clarified butter). However, it's easy to cut down on the fat and transform traditional dishes into healthy meals using clever alternatives of ingredients and techniques. Unhealthy saturated ghee can be replaced with healthy monounsaturated fats such as sunflower or olive oils, and by using a nonstick pan, you'll need to use less oil. You can use low-fat cuts of meat and remove the skin from chicken where most of its fat lies. Many high-fat ingredients used in classic Indian dishes, such as coconut milk and dairy products, can be replaced with low-fat versions, which still give rich results.

The recipes also utilize the most healthy cooking techniques, such as steaming, braising, baking, grilling and stir-frying, and abandon the less healthy alternatives. For example, samosas are traditionally deep-fried, but here they are simply brushed with a tiny amount of oil and baked until crisp and golden. The results are just as delicious as the deep-fried version and better for you.

For those who are trying to cut down on the amount of salt they eat, Indian food is the perfect choice. The generous use of spices, aromatics and other flavourings allows you to produce wonderfully tasty dishes using very little salt. A squeeze of lime juice, a little extra turmeric or a dash of tamarind water is often all that is needed to enhance and bring together the flavours of a dish. And the great thing about using less salt in cooking is that once you start using less, you'll find you don't need to use as much. You will start to enjoy the fresh, clean taste of the other ingredients and flavourings so much more.

Eating the Indian way is all about coming together and sharing food with family and friends. A traditional meal is usually just one course – a casual affair comprising a selection of dishes placed on the table at the same time, with everyone serving themselves. There will be a choice of dishes, probably one meat, poultry or fish dish, a vegetarian dish or dhal, a rice dish, a bread, a bowl of yogurt or curd and a selection of pickles and chutneys. For a vegetarian meal, the meat or fish dish will be replaced with a dhal or pulse dish to provide protein, and for a more formal occasion or for larger numbers of people, more dishes will be served.

When we go to an Indian restaurant in the West, we often enjoy appetizers followed by a selection of main dishes, then a dessert, and the recipes in this book will allow you to do just that if you want to. However, don't feel restricted by tradition – you can enjoy these dishes in any way you like. You can savour a single dish on its own rather than as part of an Indian feast. Many of the vegetable dishes make perfect accompaniments for Western-style grilled meats and fish, or when you're feeling peckish, you can select one of the snacks, such as Vegetable Samosas *(see page 28)* or Smoked Aubergine Dip *(see page 38),* or make a selection of appetizers when entertaining. The drinks, from teas to juices, are great at any time of day, with or without a meal and the desserts are just as good following a Western meal as an Indian one.

However you choose to use the recipes in this book, adopt the Indian approach to dining – and submerge yourself in the joy of preparing, cooking, sharing and eating good food.

INDIAN FLAVOURS

The essence of authentic Indian cooking lies in the ingredients you use and, in particular, in the wonderful combinations of spices, aromatics, herbs and other flavourings that are blended and cooked to produce that unmistakable taste. A well-stocked storecupboard is essential and although most of the ingredients can be found in large supermarkets, there's nothing like browsing among the shelves of Asian supermarkets and greengrocers to inspire your culinary zeal and nurture your taste for the exotic. The smell of warm spices floating in the air and the piles of glorious, fresh produce will be enough to have you running home and pulling pans out of the cupboard.

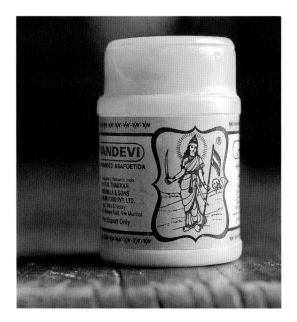

SPICES

The imaginative use of spices characterizes Indian cuisine, so keep the basics in your storecupboard. Quality is essential, so buy spices from a supplier with a rapid turnover – spices lose their flavour with age and stale spices can spoil a dish. Ground spices lose their flavour within a few months, therefore it is often better to buy whole spices and grind them as required. Some spices need to be roasted in a dry pan to bring out their aroma before grinding, while others can be used as they are.

Finally, store your spices well. They should be kept in tightly sealed containers, in a cool, dark place – and don't keep them for too long. If you find that you have very old spices in your storecupboard, it is well worth throwing them out and buying fresh ones – you'll really taste the difference.

AMCHOOR Also known as dried mango powder, this pale yellow powder made from dried green mangoes is used as a souring agent to bring out the flavour of other ingredients. Amchoor has a tart, fruity tang with a hint of sweetness and is widely available in Asian stores. If unavailable, you can use a squeeze of lemon or lime juice or a dash of tamarind water instead.

ASAFOETIDA Available in lump or ground form from Asian stores, this is a plant resin with a very strong flavour and it is used in only very small quantities to give a subtle, garlicky aroma. Store in a very tightly sealed container to retain its flavour.

CARDAMOM This sweetly aromatic spice has a gingery, citrusy, almost eucalyptus-like fragrance. It is widely used in both sweet and savoury dishes. The pods may be added whole to rice or split open and the seeds ground or used whole. The ground seeds are used in spice mixes and are a key ingredient in garam masala. Whole seeds are often chewed as a breath freshener. There are three varieties of cardamom: green, white and black. The white pods are simply bleached green pods, and have a milder flavour. The black pods, which are used only in savoury dishes, come from a related plant and have less aroma.

CASSIA Also known as Chinese cinnamon, cassia has a coarser appearance than cinnamon and a stronger flavour. If cassia is unavailable, cinnamon can be used instead. Pieces of the bark of the tree are available, or it may be ground.

CHILLI Whole dried red chillies add a fiery heat to dishes, so use with caution. They are usually fried in hot oil to intensify their flavour. Dried chilli flakes tend to have a milder flavour. Chilli powders made from dried chillies vary in heat and are often labelled hot, medium and mild. Cayenne pepper is fiery-hot, while paprika has a mild, slightly sweet, smoky flavour.

CINNAMON This sweet, warming spice is used to flavour both sweet and savoury dishes. It comes from the bark of a tree related to the laurel family and is available as sticks of rolled bark, or ground as a powder. If a cinnamon stick is used for flavouring, it should be discarded once the dish is cooked.

CLOVES These very dark brown buds of an evergreen tree have a strong, pungent flavour and are used in small quantities, either whole or ground. If whole, do not eat them once the dish is cooked

CORIANDER The pale brown seed of the coriander plant has a warm, burnt-orange aroma and may be used whole or ground. If grinding the seeds yourself, roast them first in a dry frying pan.

CUMIN Ubiquitous in Indian cooking, these small, elongated, pale brown seeds are available whole or ground. Cumin has a distinctive warm, pungent aroma and is usually fried first to intensify its flavour. Whole seeds may be roasted and sprinkled over a dish just before serving; if grinding the seeds yourself, roast them first in a dry frying pan.

CURRY LEAVES These small, dark green leaves have a distinctive 'curry' aroma and are available fresh in Asian stores. (The fresh leaves freeze well.) Dried leaves are also available, although their flavour is not as good as that of the fresh leaves. Curry leaves are usually fried first, to release their flavour.

CURRY POWDERS AND PASTES Ready-made curry powders and pastes are an invention of the West but are, nonetheless, a useful stand-by ingredient in the Indian storecupboard. They are widely available in supermarkets and Asian stores. There are many different varieties, usually labelled as mild, medium and hot, as well as more specific mixes, such as Madras curry powder or tandoori spice mix. (See separate entry for garam masala.)

FENNEL SEEDS Widely available, these small, pale greenish-brown seeds have a subtle, aniseed flavour. They are used as a flavouring in some dishes, and are often served in India after the meal as a digestive and breath freshener.

FENUGREEK These tiny, smooth, yellowish seeds are used in pickles, chutneys and vegetarian dishes.

GARAM MASALA Every Indian household has its own variation of this classic spice mix, which is usually added to a dish towards the end of cooking time. A classic mix contains cardamom, cloves, cumin, peppercorns, cinnamon and nutmeg. You can make your own at home, but very good ready-made mixes are available from supermarkets and Asian stores.

MACE This is the lacy covering of the nutmeg and is more usually available as a ground powder. It has a similar flavour to nutmeg.

MUSTARD SEEDS An essential flavouring in Indian cooking – particularly dhals, vegetarian and rice dishes, and pickles – black, brown and yellow mustard seeds are usually fried until they 'pop' to achieve a mellow, nutty flavour. The crushed, whole seeds are extremely peppery and are sometimes added to pickles.

NIGELLA Also known as black onion seeds or kalonji, these tiny, pungent seeds are most frequently used to flavour breads and pickles. They have quite a strong taste, so use them with caution.

NUTMEG Sweet and warmly aromatic, the whole spice comes as a round 'nut' that is easy to grate on the fine blade of a grater. Although ground nutmeg is widely available, it quickly loses its taste and aroma, so it is better to buy the whole spice.

PEPPERCORNS Native to the Malabar coast, these tiny, pungent berries are a very popular flavouring. They may be used whole, crushed or freshly ground. Avoid the ready-ground spice, because it loses the fresh, pungent bite of the whole spice.

SAFFRON Harvested from a special crocus grown in southern Spain and Kashmir, these deep-orange strands of the dried stamens are used to impart a wonderfully musky fragrance and rich golden colour to rice dishes and desserts. It is one of the most expensive spices, but only a little is needed and it is well worth the cost. Avoid the powdered spice; the flavour is not as good and it may well have been adulterated.

TAMARIND Used as a souring agent to bring out and enhance the flavour of other ingredients, tamarind has a sharp, fruity tang. It is obtained from a pod and is usually available as a pulp, paste or purée. The pulp needs to be soaked in hot water for several hours, then strained; the paste or purée can simply be dissolved in hot water.

TURMERIC This bright orange-yellow rhizome has a warm, musky flavour and is used in small quantities in vegetable and lentil dishes. The fresh spice can some-times be found in Asian stores, but it is usually easier to buy the ready-ground spice. The whole dried spice can also be found in Asian stores, but it is extremely hard and difficult to grind.

URAD DHAL Although this is a type of bean, in south Indian cooking urad dhal is used as a spice – fried first to release and intensify its nutty flavour.

WET SPICES AND AROMATICS

As well as the dried spices that can be found in the Indian storecupboard, there is also a selection of 'wet' spices and aromatics that can be found in the fresh vegetable sections of supermarkets and Asian stores. Always look for unblemished, crisp and fresh ingredients.

CHILLIES Fresh green and red chilli peppers are used to give heat and flavour to many Indian dishes – although it should be noted that not all Indian dishes contain chillies and many spiced dishes can be mild. If you are not used to hot food, you can reduce the quantity of chilli given in the recipe to give a milder result. Green chillies are more commonly used, although the riper red chillies do feature in many dishes. Much of the intense heat resides in the seeds and pith, so unless you want a fiery-hot dish, slit open the chillies and remove the seeds and pith before slicing or chop-ping the flesh. Always wash your hands with soap and water immediately after chopping chillies and avoid touching your eyes, nose, mouth and sensitive skin with chilli-hands or fingers – the result will be exceedingly painful and uncomfortable.

GARLIC An absolute essential in Indian cooking, garlic is used with ginger and onion as the base of many classic dishes. There is no substitute for the flavour of fresh garlic, which is usually sliced, crushed or grated and fried before other spices are added. Garlic can be grated into a paste and stored in an airtight jar in the fridge for up to 5 days.

GINGER Fresh root ginger is another indispensable aromatic and is used in both savoury and sweet dishes. It has a fresh, zesty, peppery flavour; dried ground ginger is no substitute. Look for ginger with a smooth, light brown skin and peel it before slicing and cutting it into thin slivers or dice, or grating. Store fresh ginger in the fridge for up to 2 weeks.

ONIONS Although the onion is usually classed as a vegetable, it is such an essential flavouring ingredient in authentic Indian cooking (frequently used together with garlic and fresh root ginger), that it deserves to be placed among the wet spices and aromatics. Many different types are used to different effects, including sweet yellow onions, mild red onions and spring onions. Store onions in a wire basket or a bowl in the kitchen at room temperature.

SHALLOTS These small, pungent members of the onion family are used in exactly the same way as any other onion, particularly in southern and south-western Indian cooking. The easiest way to peel shallots is to simply slice each one in half lengthways and then remove the outer skin.

HERBS

Although fresh herbs do not play as large a role as spices in Indian cooking, they are still an integral part of the cuisine and impart a clean, fresh flavour to many dishes. They are usually added towards the end of cooking time or sprinkled over the finished dish.

BAY LEAVES The whole leaves are used occasionally in curries and the dried, ground leaves are sometimes added to garam masala. In Indian, they are known as *tej patta* and are usually sold in their dried form.

CORIANDER Also known as cilantro, fresh coriander is an important ingredient in many savoury dishes, salads and chutneys. Its delicate leaves have a distinctive, fragrant aroma and are usually added to dishes just before serving.

DILL Known as *suva* in India, distinctive, aniseed-scented dill is traditionally used in lentil dishes, but it also makes a good addition to rice. Store in the fridge wrapped in dampened kitchen paper for up to a week.

MINT Fresh, zesty mint is a popular ingredient in many dishes and chutneys. Although dried mint is widely available, it does not have the same tang as the fresh herb.

STORECUPBOARD INGREDIENTS

To make cooking completely stress-free, it is important to have a well-stocked storecupboard. Visit Asian supermarkets and greengrocers for specialist Indian ingredients so that you can always substitute one ingredient for another. Re-stock regularly.

COCONUT Another essential ingredient, coconut milk and cream are added to savoury dishes to add a rich sweetness and smooth, creamy texture. Although you can make your own coconut milk from the flesh of fresh coconuts, it is much easier to use the canned variety, of which there are healthier low-fat versions. Desiccated coconut is also commonly used and is available in packets. This is available plain or sweetened.

GRAM FLOUR Also known as besan, this golden flour (which is made from ground chickpeas) has a lovely, slightly nutty flavour and is used widely for thickening and binding as well as for making batters.

GROUND RICE To be distinguished from rice flour, this is used in some Indian desserts. As it is often used in small amounts, you can make your own by grinding rice in a coffee grinder.

LENTILS, PEAS AND BEANS A plate of wholesome dhal is the staple of most Indians and a good stock of dried and canned pulses is essential for the Indian kitchen. Dried lentils, split peas and pale green mung beans need no soaking and do not take long to cook, while beans such as black-eyed beans, kidney beans and chickpeas require lengthy soaking and long boiling until tender. For these 'high maintenance' pulses, it is worth buying the canned variety to save time. Look for beans canned in water, rather than brine, and always rinse them well before adding them to the pan.

NUTS AND SEEDS These play an important role in the Indian kitchen. Ground almonds and cashew nuts are a popular addition to savoury dishes, while pale green pistachio nuts are often used in desserts. Poppy seeds are usually toasted to intensify their taste, and are used to flavour curries. White poppy seeds are mainly used to thicken curries. If using from the storecupboard, you can always dry-roast them to bring out their flavour.

OILS Although ghee (clarified butter), is the traditional fat used for Indian cooking, the recipes in this book use healthier sunflower and olive oils. These oils have a mild flavour, so they do not interfere with the subtle flavourings of the dishes.

RICE By far the best choice of rice for serving with Indian food is basmati rice. Although it is a little more expensive than other long-grain rices, it has a wonderfully fragrant aroma and light fluffy texture when cooked. It benefits from rinsing or soaking in cold water before cooking.

RICE FLOUR is used in both sweet and savoury dishes, including the classic southern pancakes, dosas and the delicate steamed cakes, idlis.

ROSEWATER This delicate, fragrant flower essence is used to flavour desserts and sweets. It can be found in most supermarkets or in Asian and Middle Eastern stores. Rose petals are sometimes used as a garnish.

SEMOLINA Coarse-ground semolina, known as *sooji* or *rava*, is available from Asian stores. It can be dry-roasted and is used to make the classic south-western dish *uppama*, which is rather like a spiced vegetable pilaf and is a traditional breakfast dish. Do not buy the fine semolina used for puddings or sweets or you will end up with a sticky mess.

SWEETENERS Indian desserts and drinks are often very sweet, but many savoury dishes also have a little sweetness to balance the other sharper flavours.

Jaggery, a form of raw, lump, cane sugar, sold in blocks or moulds is the classic Indian sugar but other sweeteners, including palm sugar and honey, are used in the recipes in this book. Jaggery and palm sugar are both available from Asian stores. Soft brown sugar can be used if jaggery and palm sugar are not available.

FRESH INGREDIENTS

The recipes in this book make use of the wonderful array of fresh ingredients available – from vibrant fruits and vegetables to fish, poultry, meat and dairy products. The ingredients used here should be easy to find – if they are not available in a regular supermarket, visit your nearest Asian grocer.

COCONUT The grated flesh of fresh coconut is called for in many recipes and some advice is needed on preparation. The easiest way to open the tough, brown-husked nut is either with a hammer or by placing the coconut in a plastic bag and bashing it hard on a concrete floor. The flesh can then be prised from the shell, the thin brown skin removed using a vegetable peeler and the remaining flesh grated. If you cannot find fresh coconut, soak desiccated coconut in hot water for 5–10 minutes and then drain it.

DAIRY PRODUCTS There are a few indispensable dairy ingredients. Yogurt is used to add creaminess to curries, as the base for marinades and dips and also as an accompaniment. Its cooling flavour is the perfect foil for hot, chilli-spiced dishes. Paneer, the fresh Indian cheese, is made from milk curds heated with lemon juice. Milk is a popular ingredient in drinks and desserts. Low-fat milk and yogurt are used in all the recipes in this book.

FRUITS These are widely used in sweet dishes, although some also play a role in savoury dishes. The juice of lemons and limes is often used to bring out the flavour of other ingredients. Green mangoes, with their crisp, savoury flesh are used as a vegetable, rather than a fruit, and dried fruits, such as dates, apricots and sultanas, are used in both desserts and tart chutneys and relishes.

VEGETABLES Many of the vegetables used in the recipes in this book are classic Indian ingredients, such as aubergines, okra (ladies' fingers), cauliflower, spinach, peas and tomatoes, while others, such as Japanese shiitake mushrooms, offer a modern twist to classic recipes.

EQUIPMENT

When it comes to preparing and making the recipes in this book, there is very little that you will need in the way of essential equipment.

THE USUAL CHOPPING BOARD AND SHARP KNIVES are needed for preparing ingredients. Be sure to use a polythene board for preparing fish, poultry and meat because they are more hygienic and easier to clean.

A MORTAR AND PESTLE are essential for grinding spices. Electric spice grinders have, however, become inexpensive and will make much quicker work of the job.

A NONSTICK FRYING PAN will prove invaluable for low-fat frying and also for dry-roasting spices. It can also be used in place of the traditional tava, the slightly concave, cast-iron griddle used for cooking flatbreads.

A HEAVY-BASED SAUCEPAN with a well-fitting lid is essential for making perfectly cooked, fluffy basmati rice.

A CHINESE WOK with a lid will also prove very useful. Its versatile shape – not unlike the traditional Indian karahi – means that it can double as a pan for healthy stir-frying, steaming or braising.

STARTERS A

ND SNACKS

ALOO CHAT

A classic snack in northern India, this piquant potato dish is traditionally eaten cold and has a fresh, tangy flavour. Pomegranate seeds make a stunning garnish and they add a lovely, clean sweet-sharp flavour to the dish.

INGREDIENTS 750 g (1½ lb) potatoes, peeled and cut into 1 cm (½ inch) cubes │ 3 tablespoons chopped coriander leaves │ 2 tablespoons chopped mint leaves │ 1 green chilli, deseeded and finely chopped │ ½ teaspoon chilli powder │ juice of 1 lemon │ 100 ml (3½ fl oz) water │ 1 red onion, very finely chopped │ salt │ pomegranate seeds, to garnish

ONE Boil the potatoes in a large saucepan of lightly salted water for 8–10 minutes or until just tender. Drain, cool thoroughly and place in a large, shallow serving dish. **TWO** Place the coriander and mint leaves, green chilli, chilli powder and lemon juice in a small food processor with the measured water and blend until fairly smooth. Pour this mixture over the potatoes and stir in the onions. Season and toss to mix well. Serve cold or at room temperature, garnished with pomegranate seeds.

Serves 4

NUTRIENT ANALYSIS PER SERVING 636 kJ – 150 kcal – 5 g protein – 34 g carbohydrate – 3 g sugars – 1 g fat – 0 g saturates – 3 g fibre – 21 mg sodium

HEALTHY TIP These tasty spiced potatoes make a much healthier snack than a bag of crisps or a couple of biscuits. They are low in fat and also offer an excellent source of slow-release energy.

recipe illustrated on pages 24–25

MINTED LAMB KEBABS

These little spiced meatballs flavoured with fresh herbs make a perfect snack to serve with drinks before dinner. Because they can be prepared ahead and popped into the oven at the last minute, they're great for quick and easy entertaining. Serve with Tamarind and Red Pepper Chutney *(see page 204)* for dipping.

INGREDIENTS 1 tablespoon chickpea flour (besan or gram flour) | 625 g (1¼ lb) finely minced lamb | 5 tablespoons finely chopped mint leaves | 3 tablespoons finely chopped coriander leaves | 2 green chillies, deseeded and finely chopped | 2 teaspoons ground cumin | 1 teaspoon ground coriander | salt and freshly ground black pepper | ½ small egg, lightly beaten | sunflower oil, to brush

ONE Place the chickpea flour, minced lamb, chopped mint and coriander leaves, green chilli and the ground spices in a mixing bowl. Season, then add the egg and, using your hands, mix until very well combined. Cover and chill for 2–3 hours or overnight if time permits.

TWO Line a large baking sheet with nonstick baking paper. Divide the lamb mixture into 12 portions and shape each one into a round ball. Flatten slightly and place on the prepared baking sheet. Brush lightly with the oil and bake in a preheated oven, 190°C (375°F), Gas Mark 5, for 12–15 minutes or until cooked through. Remove and serve immediately as an appetizer with drinks.

Serves 4

NUTRIENT ANALYSIS PER SERVING 1285 kJ – 307 kcal – 36 g protein – 3 g carbohydrate – 0 g sugars – 17 g fat – 7 g saturates – 1 g fibre – 158 mg sodium

HEALTHY TIP Lamb is quite a fatty meat, so either go for minced lamb with a low fat content or choose a low-fat cut of lamb and mince it yourself (or ask your butcher to mince it for you).

VEGETABLE SAMOSAS

These crispy pastries are classic Indian snack food – often cooked and sold on street corners, in bustling stations or carried onto trains on large trays and sold to hungry travellers. In the West, they are popularly served as an appetizer and are delicious with a light, fragrant chutney.

INGREDIENTS 1 tablespoon sunflower oil │ 1 tablespoon medium curry powder │ 1 teaspoon amchoor (dried mango powder) │ 400 g (13 oz) boiled and roughly mashed potatoes │ 100 g (3½ oz) fresh peas │ 3 tablespoons finely chopped coriander leaves │ salt │ 3 large sheets fresh filo pastry, each approx. 30 cm (12 inches) x 20 cm (8 inches) │ light olive oil, to brush

ONE Heat the sunflower oil in a large, nonstick frying pan and when hot add the curry and mango powder. Stir-fry for 10–15 seconds and then add the potatoes and peas. Stir and cook for 3–4 minutes, remove from the heat, stir in the chopped coriander, season and set aside to cool. **TWO** Line a large baking sheet with nonstick baking parchment. **THREE** Working swiftly, place the 3 sheets of filo pastry on top of each other and lay out flat on a work surface. Cut the filo pastry sheets in half widthways and then cut each half into 3 even strips to give you a total of 6 strips of filo per sheet. Lay the filo strips on a clean work surface and lightly brush each one with the olive oil. Place a teaspoon of the samosa filling at the bottom of each strip and then fold the pastry diagonally to enclose the filling and form a triangle. Press down on the pastry and fold again until you reach the end of the strip, leaving you with an enclosed filling in a triangular pastry parcel. Repeat with the remaining strips and filling to make 18 samosas. Place the samosas on the prepared baking sheet and bake for 15–20 minutes in a preheated oven, 190°C (375°F), Gas Mark 5, or until crisp and golden. Remove from the oven and serve immediately with a tomato sauce or Coriander, Coconut and Mint Chutney *(see page 207)*.

Makes 18

NUTRIENT ANALYSIS PER SAMOSA 199 kJ – 47 kcal – 1 g protein – 8 g carbohydrate – 1 g sugars – 1 g fat – 0.2 g saturates – 1 g fibre – 29 mg sodium

HEALTHY TIP Traditionally, samosas are deep-fried, but here they are simply brushed with a little oil and baked in the oven until crisp and golden. This method gives delicious results and is much healthier than the deep-fried version.

recipe illustrated on pages 30–31

CHILLED YOGURT, CUCUMBER AND MINT SOUP

Cool and refreshing yogurt soup, spiced with cumin and chilli, makes a gentle start to a spicy Indian meal. It has a slightly sharp, piquant flavour and the addition of finely chopped fresh cucumber and tomato gives it a lovely bite.

INGREDIENTS 750 ml (1¼ pints) low-fat natural yogurt, plus a little extra, to drizzle │ 750 ml (1¼ pints) fresh vegetable stock │ ½ teaspoon finely grated fresh ginger root │ ½ teaspoon ground cumin │ ¼ teaspoon chilli powder │ 1 small cucumber │ 2 plum tomatoes │ 4 tablespoons finely chopped mint leaves │ salt and freshly ground black pepper │ cumin seeds, to sprinkle

ONE Blend the yogurt, stock, ginger and spices in a food processor until smooth. Transfer to a mixing bowl. **TWO** Finely dice the cucumber; deseed and finely dice the tomatoes and stir into the yogurt mixture with the mint and seasoning. Cover and chill in the refrigerator for 30 minutes before serving drizzled with yogurt and sprinkled with roasted cumin seeds.

Serves 4

NUTRIENT ANALYSIS PER SERVING 478 kJ – 113 kcal – 10 g protein – 15 g carbohydrate – 15 g sugars – 2 g fat – 1 g saturates – 1 g fibre – 363 mg sodium

GREEN CHICKEN KEBABS

Fragrant and bursting with flavour, these succulent chicken skewers are low in fat and make an excellent light lunch or supper dish when served with a crisp cucumber and red onion salad.

INGREDIENTS 100 ml (3½ fl oz) low-fat natural yogurt | 2 garlic cloves, crushed | 2 teaspoons finely grated fresh root ginger | 2 teaspoons ground cumin | 1 teaspoon ground coriander | 1 green chilli, finely chopped | large handful of freshly chopped coriander leaves | small handful of chopped mint leaves | juice of 2 limes | sea salt | 4 chicken breasts, skinned and boned | lime halves, to serve

ONE Place the yogurt, garlic, ginger, cumin, coriander, chilli, chopped herbs and lime juice in a blender and whizz until fairly smooth. Season lightly. **TWO** Cut the chicken into bite-sized pieces and place in a large mixing bowl. Pour over the spice mixture and toss to coat evenly. Cover with clingfilm and marinate in the refrigerator for 4–6 hours or overnight if time permits. **THREE** When ready to cook, preheat the grill to medium-high and thread the chicken pieces onto 8 pre-soaked bamboo skewers. Cook under a preheated grill for 8–10 minutes, turning frequently, until cooked through and lightly browned. Remove and serve immediately with a cucumber and red onion salad with halves of lime to squeeze over.

Serves 4

NUTRIENT ANALYSIS PER SERVING 737 kJ – 175 kcal – 30 g protein – 3 g carbohydrate – 2 g sugars – 5 g fat – 1 g saturates – 0 g fibre – 118 mg sodium

HEALTHY TIP Most of the fat in chicken is found in or just under the skin, so using skinless chicken breasts is the obvious healthy option. Marinating the meat before cooking ensures that the cooked kebabs are moist and juicy despite being low in fat.

recipe illustrated on pages 36–37

SMOKED AUBERGINE DIP

Charring aubergine over an open flame before baking it gives the meltingly tender flesh a smoky flavour. The addition of hot chilli, aromatic garlic and fragrant coriander are all that are needed to make a delicious dip to serve with drinks before dinner.

INGREDIENTS 1 large, firm aubergine | 1 shallot, finely chopped | 1 garlic clove, crushed | 1 green chilli, finely chopped | 4 tablespoons chopped coriander leaves | 1 plum tomato, finely diced | 150 ml (¼ pint) low-fat natural yogurt | salt | crisp poppadums or grilled flatbreads, to serve

ONE Hold the aubergine over an open flame using long tongs (on the hob or over a barbecue) and turn and cook until the skin is blistered and charred. Transfer to a baking sheet and cook in a preheated oven, 200°C (400°F), Gas Mark 6, for 20–25 minutes or until softened. **TWO** Remove the aubergine from the oven and carefully peel off the skin over a large bowl, saving any juices. Roughly chop up the remaining flesh and place in a food processor with the saved juices. Blend until fairly smooth and then transfer to a bowl. Stir in the shallot, garlic, green chilli, coriander, tomato and yogurt. Season well and chill for 3–4 hours to allow the flavours to develop. Serve the dip with crisp poppadums or grilled flatbreads.

Serves 4

NUTRIENT ANALYSIS PER SERVING 176 kJ – 42 kcal – 3 g protein – 6 g carbohydrate – 6 g sugars – 1 g fat – 0 g saturates – 2 g fibre – 36 mg sodium

HEALTHY TIP Dips can often be high in fat, but using low-fat yogurt as the base makes this a healthy snack. If you're looking to reduce the amount of fat you eat, serve the dip with grilled flatbread, rather than deep-fried crispy poppadums.

BEETROOT AND CORIANDER SALAD

INGREDIENTS 4 large beetroot, cooked | 2 teaspoons cumin seeds | 1 teaspoon nigella seeds | 1 teaspoon coriander seeds | ¼ teaspoon mild chilli powder | 2 tablespoons half-fat coconut milk | 200 ml (7 fl oz) low-fat natural yogurt | handful of coriander leaves | 2 tablespoons roasted pumpkin seeds | sea salt

ONE Peel the beetroot and cut it into bite-sized pieces. Place in a large serving bowl. **TWO** Put a frying pan over a medium heat and place the cumin, nigella and coriander seeds in it. Dry-roast the spices for 2–3 minutes until they release their aromas. Place in a mortar and pestle and lightly crush them. Transfer to a small mixing bowl with the chilli powder, coconut milk and yogurt. Stir to mix well. **THREE** Roughly chop the coriander leaves and add to the beetroot with the pumpkin seeds. Drizzle over the yogurt mixture, season and serve immediately.

Serves 4

NUTRIENT ANALYSIS PER SERVING 394 kJ – 93 kcal – 5 g protein – 13 g carbohydrate – 11 g sugars – 3 g fat – 1 g saturates – 3 g fibre – 120 mg sodium

HEALTHY TIP Beetroot is high in antioxidants, making it excellent for boosting the immune system, fighting infection and detoxifying your body, and is also a good source of iron.

TOMATO, MIXED SPROUTS AND CUCUMBER SALAD

Mixed sprouts are widely available from any good greengrocer or health food store. They come in various mixtures from sprouted mung beans, to red lentil and chickpea sprouts and have a crisp, refreshing texture when they are used raw in salads.

INGREDIENTS 200 g (7 oz) pomodorino or cherry tomatoes, roughly chopped │ 625 g (1¼ lb) mixed fresh sprouted beans and lentils │ 1 small red onion, very finely diced │ 4 small Lebanese cucumbers, thinly sliced or finely chopped │ 1 tablespoon light olive oil │ juice of 1 lemon │ 1 teaspoon roasted cumin seeds │ 3 tablespoons chopped mint leaves │ 2 tablespoons chopped coriander leaves │ salt and freshly ground black pepper

ONE Place the tomatoes in a mixing bowl. Rinse and drain the mixed sprouts and add them to the tomatoes with the red onion and cucumber. **TWO** Mix together the olive oil, lemon juice and cumin seeds and pour over the salad. Stir in the chopped herbs and season well before serving.

Serves 4

NUTRIENT ANALYSIS PER SERVING 405 kJ – 97 kcal – 6 g protein – 10 g carbohydrate – 7 g sugars – 4 g fat – 1 g saturates – 10 g fibre – 16 mg sodium

HEALTHY TIP Sprouted beans and lentils are packed with health-giving minerals and vitamins, and sprouting actually appears to boost the nutritional content of some beans and lentils.

recipe illustrated on pages 44–45

PANEER KACHUMBER

This traditional, refreshing salad combines fresh and zesty flavours with the mild Indian cheese, paneer. Paneer is widely available in large supermarkets and Asian stores, although it can easily be made at home, simply by heating milk with a little lemon juice, then separating out and pressing the curds.

INGREDIENTS 2 x 250 g (8 oz) packs paneer (Indian cheese made from milk) │ sunflower oil, for brushing

KACHUMBER 2 plum tomatoes, deseeded and very finely chopped │ 1 bottled roasted red pepper (100 g [3½ oz]), drained and very finely chopped │ 1 shallot, peeled and very finely diced │ 50 g (2 oz) sprouted mung beans │ 4 tablespoons very finely diced cucumber │ 3 tablespoons finely chopped coriander leaves │ 1 teaspoon finely grated lime rind │ juice of 2 limes │ 1 tablespoon sunflower oil or light olive oil │ 1 teaspoon clear honey │ salt and chilli powder, to season │ coriander leaves, to garnish

ONE Cut the paneer into bite-sized cubes. Brush lightly with oil. Heat a nonstick, ridged griddle pan over a high heat and cook the paneer cubes in batches for 1–2 minutes on all sides. Remove from the heat and transfer to 4 warmed serving plates and keep warm.

TWO Place the tomatoes, red pepper, shallot, mung beans, cucumber and coriander in a small bowl. Mix together the lime rind and juice, oil and honey and pour over the vegetable mixture. Season with salt and chilli powder and toss to mix well. Spoon this mixture over and around each serving of griddled paneer, garnish with fresh coriander leaves and serve warm or at room temperature.

Serves 4

NUTRIENT ANALYSIS PER SERVING 694 kJ – 165 kcal – 17 g protein – 8 g carbohydrate – 8 g sugars – 8 g fat – 3 g saturates – 2 g fibre – 438 mg sodium

HEALTHY TIP Paneer is an excellent source of calcium, which is essential for healthy bones and teeth. It is also a good source of protein, so makes a nutritious choice for vegetarians.

recipe illustrated on pages 48–49

BARBECUED CORN WITH CHILLI AND LIME

Char-grilling corn gives it a smoky flavour, which is set off by the spicy chilli and sharp, tangy lime juice. Served piping hot, it makes a perfect snack to serve with drinks.

INGREDIENTS 4 ears of corn (or corn-on-the-cob) │ 1 tablespoon coarse chilli powder │ 1 tablespoon sea salt │ 2 limes, halved

ONE Remove the husks from the corn and reserve. **TWO** Mix together the coarse chilli powder and sea salt and place on a small plate or saucer. Cut the limes in half and set aside. **THREE** Cook the corn over a medium heat over a barbecue or under a medium hot grill for 4–5 minutes, turning them around so that they cook all over, until the corn is lightly charred in places. Remove from the heat, dip a lime half in the chilli mixture and squeeze and spread it over the corn to coat evenly. Repeat with the remaining corn, lime and chilli mixture. Place the corn on the reserved husks and eat immediately.

Serves 4

NUTRIENT ANALYSIS PER SERVING 206 kJ – 49 kcal – 2 g protein – 9 g carbohydrate – 1 g sugars – 1 g fat – 0.1 g saturates – 2 g fibre – 1964 mg sodium

MEAT AND

POULTRY

GRILLED SPICY CHICKEN

INGREDIENTS 4 chicken breast fillets, skinned | juice of 1 lemon | sea salt

MARINADE 1 teaspoon amchoor (dried mango powder) | 1 teaspoon crushed fenugreek seeds | 1 teaspoon garam masala | 2 teaspoons finely grated fresh root ginger | 2 teaspoons finely grated garlic | 1 tablespoon chilli powder | 1 teaspoon ground cumin | 1 teaspoon ground coriander | 200 ml (7 fl oz) low-fat natural yogurt | lime wedges, to serve

ONE Slit each breast diagonally, 3–4 times and place in a shallow, non-reactive dish. Squeeze over the lemon juice and season with salt. Cover and set aside. **TWO** Place all the marinade ingredients in a food processor and blend until smooth. Pour over the chicken, cover and marinate in the refrigerator for 2–3 hours. **THREE** When you are ready to cook, remove the chicken breasts from the marinade and place them on a grill rack. Cook under a medium-hot grill for 15 minutes, turning them halfway through or until they are cooked and lightly charred. Serve immediately with a crisp salad and serve garnished with lime wedges.

Serves 4

NUTRIENT ANALYSIS PER SERVING 911 kJ – 216 kcal – 36 g protein – 6 g carbohydrate – 5 g sugars – 6 g fat – 2 g saturates – 0 g fibre – 175 mg sodium

HEALTHY TIP Grilling is a really healthy cooking method because it requires no extra fat and the thick yogurt marinade ensures the chicken stays moist during cooking.

SOUTH INDIAN PEPPER CHICKEN

Spiced with peppercorns rather than chilli, this creamy curry will be popular with the whole family. Fresh ginger and garlic give it a warming, spicy aroma. Serve with a refreshing salad to complement the rich sauce.

INGREDIENTS 1 tablespoon sunflower oil │ 1 bay leaf │ 4 cloves │ ½ teaspoon crushed cardamom seeds │ 2 teaspoons crushed black peppercorns │ 1 teaspoon finely grated fresh root ginger │ 2 teaspoons finely grated garlic │ 625 g (1¼ lb) boneless, skinless chicken breasts, cut into bite-sized pieces │ 150 ml (¼ pint) water or chicken stock │ ½ teaspoon turmeric │ 350 ml (12 fl oz) low-fat natural yogurt │ salt

ONE Heat the oil in a large nonstick frying pan and when hot add the bay leaf, cloves, crushed cardamom seeds and peppercorns. Stir-fry for 30 seconds, then add the ginger, garlic and the chicken. Stir-fry over a medium heat for 4–5 minutes before adding the water or stock and the turmeric. Season. **TWO** Bring to the boil, cover, reduce the heat and simmer gently for 10–12 minutes or until the chicken is tender and cooked through. Remove from the heat, drizzle over the yogurt so that it is partially stirred in and serve.

Serves 4

NUTRIENT ANALYSIS PER SERVING 1119 kJ – 266 kcal – 40 g protein – 7 g carbohydrate – 7 g sugars – 9 g fat – 2 g saturates – 0 g fibre – 190 mg sodium

HEALTHY TIP Adding low-fat yogurt gives this dish a rich creaminess, with none of the fat that comes with cream, ground almonds or coconut – which are all popular ingredients in many Indian curries.

recipe illustrated on pages 60–61

GREEN CHICKEN CURRY

INGREDIENTS 1 tablespoon sunflower oil | 1 onion, finely chopped | 3 garlic cloves, finely chopped | 2 teaspoons grated fresh root ginger | large handful of coriander leaves, chopped | 4 tablespoons chopped mint leaves | 1 green chilli, chopped | ¼ teaspoon crushed cardamom seeds | 2 teaspoons ground cumin | 2 teaspoons ground coriander | 1 teaspoon grated jaggery or palm sugar | 400 ml (14 fl oz) half-fat coconut milk | 625 g (1¼ lb) boneless, skinless chicken thighs, cut into small pieces | 200 ml (7 fl oz) water | salt and freshly ground black pepper | Lebanese cucumber, cut into fine strips, to garnish

ONE Heat the oil in a large saucepan or wok, add the onion and cook over a medium heat for 5–6 minutes, stirring. **TWO** Meanwhile, place the garlic, ginger, herbs, green chilli, spices, jaggery and coconut milk in a food processor and blend until smooth. **THREE** Add the chicken to the onion and cook over a high heat for 4–5 minutes, until sealed and lightly browned. Pour in the coconut mixture and add the water. Season and bring to the boil. Reduce the heat, cover and cook gently for 20–25 minutes or until the chicken is tender and cooked through. Serve immediately with the garnish and steamed basmati rice.

Serves 4

NUTRIENT ANALYSIS PER SERVING 1436 kJ – 344 kcal – 31 g protein – 10 g carbohydrate – 8 g sugars – 20 g fat – 9 g saturates – 1 g fibre – 250 mg sodium

MARINATED SPICED LAMB

Spice-coated racks of lamb, baked until tender and then cut into 'cutlets', make an impressive main dish.

INGREDIENTS 4 French-trimmed racks of lamb (each rack with 3–4 ribs) │ 3 garlic cloves, crushed │ 2 teaspoons finely grated fresh root ginger │ 2 tablespoons white wine vinegar │ 6 tablespoons very finely chopped mint leaves │ 2 teaspoons ground cumin │ 2 teaspoons ground coriander │ 1 teaspoon chilli powder │ 150 ml (¼ pint) low-fat natural yogurt │ salt

ONE Place the racks of lamb in a shallow, nonreactive dish in a single layer. Put the garlic, ginger, vinegar, mint, cumin, coriander, chilli powder and yogurt in a food processor and blend until smooth. Season, then pour this mixture over the lamb to coat it evenly. Cover and chill in the refrigerator for 3–4 hours or overnight if time permits. **TWO** Lay the lamb on a nonstick baking sheet and place it in a preheated oven, 200°C (400°F), Gas Mark 6, and cook for 20–25 minutes or longer if you prefer it well done. Remove from the oven, cover with foil and allow the lamb to stand and rest for 5–10 minutes before cutting it into 'cutlets' and serving with Spiced Lemon Rice *(see page 152)*.

Serves 4

NUTRIENT ANALYSIS PER SERVING 1797 kJ – 432 kcal – 42 g protein – 4 g carbohydrate – 3 g sugars – 28 g fat – 14 g saturates – 0 g fibre – 133 mg sodium

HEALTHY TIP Marinating meat before cooking not only imparts a wonderful flavour, but also ensures moist, juicy results. Oil-based marinades can introduce extra fat, but this one, using low-fat yogurt, keeps down the fat content of the dish.

recipe illustrated on pages 66–67

BEEF KOFTA CURRY

Small, spicy balls of minced beef cooked in a smooth, spicy sauce make a warming supper. Serve with with Indian flatbreads and a fresh Indian salad or salsa. Wrap the koftas and salad up in the bread for an informal meal.

INGREDIENTS 625 g (1¼ lb) lean minced beef | 1 teaspoon finely grated fresh root ginger | 2 teaspoons fennel seeds | 1 teaspoon ground cinnamon | 1 teaspoon turmeric | 2 tablespoons mild curry powder | 500 ml (17 fl oz) tomato passata | salt and freshly ground black pepper | low-fat yogurt and mint leaves to garnish

ONE Place the mince and ginger in a large mixing bowl. Roughly crush the fennel seeds in a mortar and pestle and add to the mixture with the cinnamon. Season and, using your hands, mix thoroughly. Form the mixture into small, walnut-sized balls and set aside. **TWO** Place the turmeric, curry powder and passata in a wide, nonstick saucepan and bring to the boil. Season, reduce the heat and carefully place the meatballs in the sauce. Cover and cook gently for 15–20 minutes, stirring and turning the meatballs around occasionally, until they are cooked through. Remove from the heat, drizzle with the low-fat yogurt and scatter with the mint leaves. Serve with chapattis or other flatbreads and salad.

Serves 4

NUTRIENT ANALYSIS PER SERVING 893 kJ – 212 kcal – 32 g protein – 5 g carbohydrate – 4 g sugars – 7 g fat – 3 g saturates – 1 g fibre – 142 mg sodium

BEEF BROCHETTES WITH MANGO SALSA

Chunky beef skewers, marinated overnight, then grilled and served with a fresh salsa make a delicious lunch or supper dish. To make a substantial meal of it, serve the brochettes with a crunchy salad or salsa and chapattis for wrapping around the spicy chunks of meat.

INGREDIENTS 500 g (1 lb) beef fillet, cut into bite-sized cubes

MARINADE 150 ml (¼ pint) low-fat yogurt | ½ small onion, roughly chopped | 2 teaspoons finely grated fresh root ginger | 2 teaspoons finely grated garlic | 3 tablespoons tomato purée | 1 tablespoon medium curry powder | 2 tablespoons chopped coriander leaves | ½ teaspoon salt

SALSA 1 ripe mango, finely diced | ½ small red onion, finely diced | 2 tablespoons each of chopped coriander and mint leaves | 1 red chilli, deseeded and finely chopped | juice of 2 limes | salt

ONE Place the beef in a nonreactive bowl. Blend all the marinade ingredients together in a food processor until smooth and pour over the meat. Cover and marinate overnight in the refrigerator. **TWO** Make the salsa by combining all the ingredients in a bowl and seasoning to taste. **THREE** Thread the marinated meat on to 8 metal skewers (or pre-soaked bamboo ones) and cook under a hot grill for 12–15 minutes turning halfway through cooking until the meat is cooked to your liking. Remove and allow to rest for 3–4 minutes before serving with the mango salsa.

Serves 4

NUTRIENT ANALYSIS PER SERVING 949 kJ – 225 kcal – 29 g protein – 13 g carbohydrate – 12 g sugars – 7 g fat – 3 g saturates – 1 g fibre – 167 mg sodium

HEALTHY TIP Beef is a great source of iron, which is essential for healthy red blood cells. The cut used here is low in fat and tender.

recipe illustrated on pages 72–73

PORK KHEEMA WITH PEAS

Warm fragrant coriander, aromatic garlic and spicy chillies are the perfect partners for mildly flavoured pork.

INGREDIENTS 1 tablespoon sunflower oil | 2 garlic cloves, finely chopped | 2 green chillies, deseeded and finely chopped | 1 teaspoon ground coriander | 500 g (1 lb) minced pork | 400 g (13 oz) fresh or frozen peas | 3 tablespoons medium curry paste | 3 tablespoons tomato purée | 2 tomatoes, finely chopped | 1 teaspoon golden caster sugar | 250 ml (8 fl oz) boiling water | 2 tablespoons low-fat natural yogurt | large handful of chopped coriander leaves | salt

ONE Heat the oil in a large, nonstick wok or frying pan and when it is hot add the garlic, chillies, ground coriander and pork. Stir-fry over a high heat for 4–5 minutes until the meat is lightly browned. **TWO** Stir in the peas, curry paste, tomato purée, chopped tomatoes and sugar. Cook for 3–4 minutes and then add the measured water. Bring to the boil, cover, reduce the heat and cook gently for 8–10 minutes or until the meat is tender. Remove from the heat, stir in the yogurt and chopped coriander and season.

Serves 4

NUTRIENT ANALYSIS PER SERVING 1513 kJ – 362 kcal – 35 g protein – 18 g carbohydrate – 10 g sugars – 17 g fat – 4 g saturates – 8 g fibre – 449 mg sodium

FISH AND S

EAFOOD

CRISPY GRILLED RED MASALA MACKEREL

INGREDIENTS 4 fresh mackerel, each around 250–300 g (8–10 oz), cleaned and gutted

RED MASALA PASTE 1 tablespoon sunflower oil | 1 teaspoon finely grated fresh root ginger | 2 teaspoons finely grated garlic | 2 red chillies, deseeded and very finely chopped | 1 teaspoon chilli powder | ½ teaspoon turmeric | 1 teaspoon ground cumin | 1 teaspoon ground coriander | 4 tablespoons tomato purée | 1 teaspoon grated jaggery or palm sugar | juice of 2 lemons | salt

TO SERVE red onion rings, sliced cucumber and sliced tomatoes

ONE Make 4–5 deep diagonal slices on each side of the fish. **TWO** Make the paste by placing all the ingredients in a food processor with a couple of tablespoons of water and mix until fairly smooth. Season well and spread over the fish, making sure it gets into the slits. **THREE** Cook under a hot grill for 6–8 minutes on each side until cooked through and lightly charred at the edges. Serve immediately with the red onion rings, sliced cucumber and sliced tomatoes.

Serves 4

NUTRIENT ANALYSIS PER SERVING 1676 kJ – 403 kcal – 31 g protein – 7 g carbohydrate – 5 g sugars – 28 g fat – 5 g saturates – 0 g fibre – 265 mg sodium

HEALTHY TIP The spices in this masala have many therapeutic properties, including boosting the immune system, improving circulation, improving mood and reducing inflammation.

MUSTARD-GRILLED SARDINES

Perfect for a summer barbecue or a simple lunch or supper, these deliciously spicy sardines are great served simply with a fresh, crunchy salad and lemon wedges for squeezing over.

INGREDIENTS 12 medium-sized sardines | 1 tablespoon wholegrain mustard | juice of 2 lemons | 1 teaspoon chilli powder | 1 teaspoon garam masala | salt | lemon wedges, to serve

ONE Put the sardines on a large work surface and using a sharp knife, make 2–3 diagonal slashes on both sides of each fish. **TWO** In a small bowl, mix together the mustard, lemon juice, chilli powder and garam masala. Season, then spread this mixture over the fish. **THREE** Place the sardines on a grill rack and cook under a medium-hot grill for 3–4 minutes on each side or until cooked through. Serve hot with wedges of lemon.

Serves 4

NUTRIENT ANALYSIS PER SERVING 1078 kJ – 257 kcal – 32 g protein – 1 g carbohydrate – 1 g sugars – 14 g fat – 4 g saturates – 0 g fibre – 249 mg sodium

HEALTHY TIP Sardines are oily fish, which offer a great source of health-giving omega-3 essential fatty acids. You should aim to eat oily fish at least once a week to ensure that you consume an adequate amount of this valuable nutrient.

BENGALI-STYLE MUSTARD FISH

In Bengal in eastern India, there is a plentiful supply of fish from the Bay of Bengal, and many different ways of cooking it. Here, white fish is simply spiced with mustard, turmeric and chilli and baked until just cooked through.

INGREDIENTS 1 teaspoon turmeric │ 1 teaspoon chilli powder │ 2 tablespoons wholegrain mustard │ 2 teaspoons black mustard seeds │ 2 tablespoons sunflower oil │ juice of 1 lime │ salt │ 4 thick halibut or cod fillets, each about 250 g (8 oz), skinned │ chopped coriander leaves, to garnish

ONE Line a baking sheet with nonstick baking paper. **TWO** Using a mortar and pestle, crush the turmeric, chilli powder, wholegrain mustard and black mustard seeds until fairly well combined. Add the oil and lime juice and season well. Stir to mix thoroughly. **THREE** Place the fish fillets on the prepared baking sheet. Spread the mustard mixture over the fish and put it into a preheated oven, 200°C (400°F), Gas Mark 6, and cook for 15–20 minutes or until cooked through. Remove from the oven and serve immediately, garnished with chopped coriander.

Serves 4

NUTRIENT ANALYSIS PER SERVING 958 kJ – 228 kcal – 32 g protein – 1 g carbohydrate – 0 g sugars – 11 g fat – 1 g saturates – 0 g fibre – 274 mg sodium

MANGO AND PRAWN CURRY

Rich and full-flavoured, this spicy curry from Goa offers the perfect balance of sweet and sharp, spicy and creamy and smooth and chunky. The green mango, used here as a vegetable, gives the curry a great texture.

INGREDIENTS 1 teaspoon chilli powder | 1 teaspoon paprika | ½ teaspoon turmeric | 3 garlic cloves, crushed | 2 teaspoons finely grated fresh root ginger | 2 tablespoons ground coriander | 2 teaspoons ground cumin | 1 tablespoon grated jaggery or palm sugar | 400 ml (14 fl oz) water | 1 green mango, stoned and thinly sliced | 400 ml (14 fl oz) half-fat coconut milk | 1 tablespoon tamarind paste | 1 kg (2 lb) raw tiger prawns, cleaned and deveined | salt

ONE Put the chilli powder, paprika, turmeric, garlic, ginger, ground coriander, cumin and jaggery into a large wok with the measured water and stir to mix well. Place over a high heat and bring the mixture to the boil. Reduce the heat and cook covered for 8–10 minutes. **TWO** Add the mango, coconut milk and tamarind paste and stir to combine. Bring the mixture back to the boil and add the prawns. **THREE** Stir and cook gently for 8–10 minutes or until all the prawns have turned pink and are cooked through. Season and serve the curry with steamed basmati rice.

Serves 4

NUTRIENT ANALYSIS PER SERVING 1070 kJ – 255 kcal – 24 g protein – 18 g carbohydrate – 14 g sugars – 10 g fat – 6 g saturates – 1 g fibre – 372 mg sodium

HEALTHY TIP Although prawns contain cholesterol, it is saturated fats that are the real villain. The liver turns saturated fats into cholesterol in the body, thus raising your overall cholesterol levels. Prawns are low in saturated fats and have many other health benefits, so most health professionals agree that it's fine to eat them, even if you're trying to reduce your cholesterol levels.

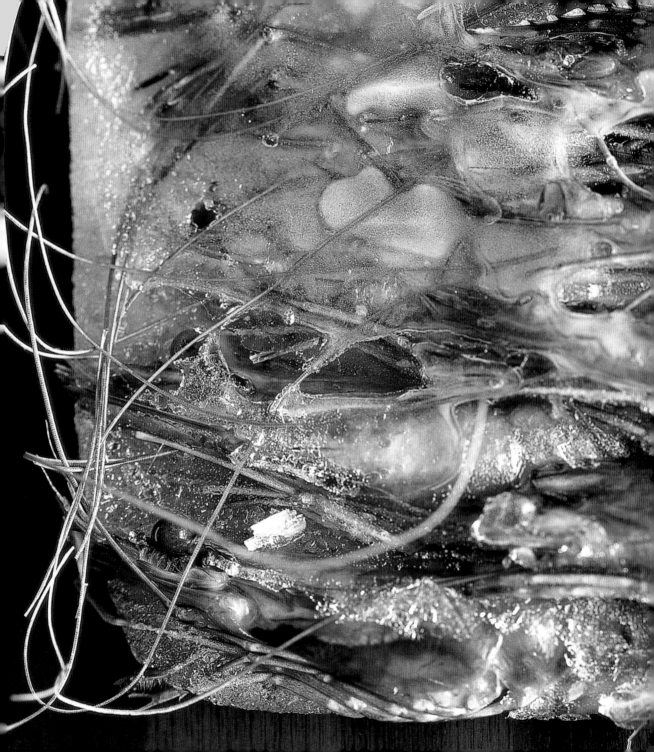

BOMBAY-STYLE FISH

Fish cooked simply in a rich spice paste makes a quick and tasty dish. Serve with light, fresh vegetable accompaniments and plain steamed or boiled rice to offer a good balance of contrasting textures and flavours.

INGREDIENTS 1 teaspoon cardamom seeds | 1 teaspoon fennel seeds | 2 teaspoons coriander seeds | 1 teaspoon cumin seeds | 2 strands mace | 1 teaspoon white poppy seeds | 65 g (2½ oz) cashew nuts, roasted and chopped | 40 g (1½ oz) desiccated coconut | 1 red onion, finely chopped | 3 garlic cloves, chopped | 2 green chillies, deseeded and chopped | large handful of chopped coriander leaves | 2 tablespoons chopped mint leaves | juice of 2 limes | 1 tablespoon sunflower oil | 200 ml (7 fl oz) water | 1 large pomfret, cleaned and cut into 4 thick steaks or 4 thick 200 g (7 oz) cod fillets | red chillies, finely chopped, to garnish

ONE In a small frying pan, dry-roast the cardamom seeds, fennel seeds, coriander seeds, cumin seeds and mace for a few minutes over a medium heat until aromatic. Remove from the heat and transfer to a coffee grinder, add the poppy seeds and grind to a fine powder. **TWO** Place the cashew nuts and coconut in a frying pan and roast for a few minutes over a medium heat until the coconut is lightly coloured. Transfer to a food processor with the spice mix, red onion, garlic, green chilli, coriander leaves, mint leaves and the lime juice. Blend to form a paste. **THREE** Heat the oil in a large, nonstick frying pan and add the spice paste. Stir and fry for 1–2 minutes over a high heat and then add the measured water. Stir to mix well, bring to the boil and then gently lay the fish fillets across the bottom of the pan. **FOUR** Reduce the heat to medium and simmer gently for 8–10 minutes or until the fish is cooked through. Garnish with finely chopped red chillies and serve immediately with poppadums, sago snacks or basmati rice.

Serves 4

NUTRIENT ANALYSIS PER SERVING 1475 kJ – 353 kcal – 40 g protein – 8 g carbohydrate – 4 g sugars – 19 g fat – 7 g saturates – 3 g fibre – 164 mg sodium

HEALTHY TIP Dry-roasting the spices, cashew nuts and coconut in a clean frying pan helps to bring out their flavour, without adding extra fat.

recipe illustrated on pages 92–93

TANDOORI FISH KEBABS

Dishes cooked in a tandoor clay oven have a very distinctive flavour. This version, using a classic yogurt-based marinade with traditional spices, and the fish then grilled until just cooked through, is equally good.

INGREDIENTS 4 trout fillets, each about 150 g (5 oz), skinned

TANDOORI MARINADE 200 g (7 oz) low-fat natural yogurt | 3 garlic cloves, crushed | 1 teaspoon finely grated fresh root ginger | 1 tablespoon tandoori spice mix | juice of 1 lemon | salt

ONE Trim the trout fillets and place them in a wide, nonreactive bowl in a single layer. Mix together all the ingredients for the marinade, season and spread this mixture all over the fish. Cover and allow to marinate for 15–20 minutes if time permits. **TWO** Thread 2 presoaked bamboo skewers through each fillet and arrange them on a grill rack. Place under a preheated medium-hot grill and cook for 4–5 minutes on each side or until cooked through. Remove from the grill and serve hot, with flatbreads and salad.

Serves 4

NUTRIENT ANALYSIS PER SERVING 870 kJ – 207 kcal – 32 g protein – 5 g carbohydrate – 4 g sugars – 7 g fat – 0 g saturates – 0 g fibre – 128 mg sodium

HEALTHY TIP Trout contain a plentiful supply of omega-3 fatty acids, which are believed to improve heart health, fight against cancer and even improve the condition of your skin.

MASALA FENNEL PRAWNS

Fresh, juicy prawns, cooked simply in a fennel-spiced sauce, makes for a healthy lunch when served with rice and a chopped salad.

INGREDIENTS 1 teaspoon light olive oil | 10–12 fresh curry leaves | 2 large shallots, halved and finely sliced | 2 teaspoons finely grated garlic | 1 teaspoon finely grated fresh root ginger | 1 tablespoon fennel seeds | 1 tablespoon mild curry powder | 5 large, ripe tomatoes, deseeded and chopped | 750 g (1½ lb) raw tiger prawns, peeled and deveined | sea salt | coriander leaves, to garnish

ONE Heat the oil in a large wok or nonstick frying pan and add the curry leaves. Stir-fry for 30 seconds and add the shallots. Stir and fry over a medium heat for 4–5 minutes, then add the garlic, ginger and fennel seeds. **TWO** Cook gently for 2–3 minutes, then add the curry powder and tomatoes. Turn the heat to high and stir-fry the mixture for 3–4 minutes. **THREE** Add the prawns and cook over a high heat for 6–7 minutes or until the prawns turn pink and are just cooked through. Remove from the heat, season and garnish with fresh coriander leaves. Serve immediately with steamed rice.

Serves 4

NUTRIENT ANALYSIS PER SERVING 599 kJ – 142 kcal – 18 g protein – 8 g carbohydrate – 6 g sugars – 5 g fat – 1 g saturates – 3 g fibre – 202 mg sodium

HERBED SPICED PRAWN PARCELS

Steaming prawns inside little foil parcels is one of the healthiest ways of cooking them. Coating the prawns first in a paste of coconut milk and spices gives them a rich, rounded flavour.

INGREDIENTS 875 g (1¾ lb) raw tiger prawns, cleaned and deveined

HERBED SPICE PASTE 2 garlic cloves, finely chopped | 1 teaspoon finely grated fresh root ginger | 4 spring onions, finely chopped | 6 tablespoons chopped coriander leaves | 200 ml (7 fl oz) half-fat coconut milk | 1 red chilli, chopped | 1 teaspoon ground cumin | ½ teaspoon garam masala | ¼ teaspoon turmeric | finely grated rind and juice of 1 lime | 1 teaspoon grated jaggery or palm sugar | salt

ONE Place the prawns in a wide, shallow dish. **TWO** Put all the ingredients for the paste mixture into a food processor and blend until you have a coarse purée. Spoon this mixture over the prawns and toss to coat them evenly. **THREE** Make 4 squares of doubled-sided foil 30 cm (12 inches) square and divide the prawn mixture between them. To seal the prawns in, make a parcel by bringing the edges of the foil together and crimping them together. **FOUR** Lay the parcels on a baking sheet and place it in a preheated oven, 200°C (400°F), Gas Mark 6, and cook for 15–20 minutes or until the prawns have turned pink and are cooked through. Remove the parcels from the oven, place each one on a plate and serve immediately; open the parcels at the table.

Serves 4

NUTRIENT ANALYSIS PER SERVING 635 kJ – 152 kcal – 19 g protein – 6 g carbohydrate – 4 g sugars – 6 g fat – 3 g saturates – 0 g fibre – 246 mg sodium

HEALTHY TIP Garlic, one of the essential flavourings in Indian cooking, has many health-giving properties. It's a natural anti-bacterial and is also believed to help protect against certain forms of cancer and boost the immune system.

recipe illustrated on pages 104–105

GOAN-STYLE CLAMS AND MUSSELS

Goa, on the western shore of India, offers a rich source of inspiration for preparing fish and shellfish. Here, fresh clams and mussels are steamed with a rich blend of warm spices, then tossed with sweet grated coconut and fragrant coriander to make an utterly more-ish dish.

INGREDIENTS 1 tablespoon sunflower oil | 2 shallots, very finely sliced | 1 red chilli, slit lengthways | 1 teaspoon finely grated fresh root ginger | 2 garlic cloves, finely chopped | 2 plum tomatoes, finely chopped | 1 teaspoon garam masala | ½ teaspoon turmeric | 625 g (1¼ lb) fresh clams, scrubbed | 1 kg (2 lb) fresh mussels, scrubbed | 200 g (7 oz) fresh grated coconut | 6–8 tablespoons chopped coriander leaves

TO SERVE wedges of lime or lemon | crusty bread

ONE Heat the oil in a large wok or saucepan. Add the shallots, red chilli, ginger and garlic and stir-fry over a high heat for 2–3 minutes. Add the tomatoes, garam masala and turmeric and continue to cook for 3–4 minutes, stirring often. **TWO** Tip in the clams and mussels, stir to mix and cover tightly. Continue to cook over a high heat for 6–8 minutes or until the clams and mussels have opened. Discard any that remain closed. **THREE** Stir in the grated coconut and coriander and mix well. Serve in large individual bowls with wedges of lemon or lime to squeeze over. Eat with your fingers and have plenty of crusty bread on hand to mop up any juices.

Serves 4

NUTRIENT ANALYSIS PER SERVING 1266 kJ – 304 kcal – 20 g protein – 5 g carbohydrate – 4 g sugars – 23 g fat – 16 g saturates – 7 g fibre – 232 mg sodium

HEALTHY TIP Shellfish are a useful source of zinc, which plays an important role in the body's growth, immunity and reproductive functions.

recipe illustrated on pages 108–109

CREAMY FISH KORMA

Delicately flavoured korma curries are usually enriched with cream and ground almonds, but here half-fat coconut milk and very low-fat fromage frais are used instead. The final result is just as good and really makes the most of fresh cod.

INGREDIENTS 750 g (1½ lb) thick cod fillet, skinned and cut into bite-sized cubes | 2 tablespoons plain flour | 2 tablespoons light olive oil | 1 onion, halved and thinly sliced | 2 garlic cloves crushed | 1 teaspoon turmeric | 1 green chilli, finely chopped | 2 tablespoons lemon juice | 200 ml (7 fl oz) half-fat coconut milk | 100 ml (3½ fl oz) very low-fat natural fromage frais

ONE Lightly coat the fish with flour, patting away any excess. Heat the oil in a large, nonstick frying pan over a medium heat and add the fish. Fry the fish for 2–3 minutes on each side. Remove from the pan with a slotted spoon and set aside. **TWO** Add the onion to the pan and stir-fry over a medium heat for 5–6 minutes. Add the garlic, turmeric, chilli and lemon juice and stir and fry for another 2–3 minutes. Stir in the coconut milk, bring to the boil and then reduce the heat and stir and simmer gently for 8–10 minutes. **THREE** Return the fish to the pan, spoon the sauce over the fish and cook for 4–5 minutes until heated through. Remove from the heat and gently stir in the fromage frais before serving.

Serves 4

NUTRIENT ANALYSIS PER SERVING 1324 kJ – 315 kcal – 39 g protein – 15 g carbohydrate – 6 g sugars – 12 g fat – 4 g saturates – 1 g fibre – 219 mg sodium

VEGETABLES

OKRA WITH TOMATO AND CUCUMBER

People are often nervous of cooking okra owing to its slightly sticky texture, but it is simple to cook well and once you have tried this tasty recipe, it is sure to become a regular dish in your repertoire.

INGREDIENTS 400 g (13 oz) fresh okra │ 2 tablespoons sunflower oil │ 2 tablespoons mustard seeds │ 2 dried red chillies (whole) │ 1 onion, very finely sliced │ 2 plum tomatoes, roughly chopped │ 1 small cucumber, roughly chopped │ 1 garlic clove, very finely chopped │ 1 teaspoon very finely chopped fresh root ginger │ ½ teaspoon turmeric │ salt │ freshly grated coconut, to sprinkle

ONE Slice the okra diagonally into 1 cm (½ inch) slices. Heat the oil in a large, nonstick frying pan and when hot add the mustard seeds. As they begin to 'pop', add the dried red chillies and onion. **TWO** Stir-fry and cook over a medium heat for 4–5 minutes until the onion has softened, then stir in the tomatoes, cucumber, garlic, ginger and turmeric. Stir-fry for another 3–4 minutes and then turn the heat to high and add the sliced okra. Stir-fry for 2–3 minutes, season and remove from the heat. **THREE** Sprinkle over the grated coconut and serve immediately.

Serves 4

NUTRIENT ANALYSIS PER SERVING 617 kJ – 149 kcal – 5 g protein – 10 g carbohydrate – 7 g sugars – 10 g fat – 3 g saturates – 6 g fibre – 17 mg sodium

HEALTHY TIP You should aim to eat five portions of fruit and vegetables a day, covering a good range of different types. Include this dish as part of a meal, and you'll be well on your way to your daily quota.

recipe illustrated on pages 118–119

LIME POTATOES WITH COURGETTES

Potatoes and courgettes are a classic combination in Indian cooking. The addition of zingy lime juice and fragrant fresh herbs really sets them off. Serve with Indian breads for scooping up the spiced potatoes.

INGREDIENTS 1 tablespoon sunflower oil | 1 small onion, finely diced | 2 teaspoons cumin seeds | 2 garlic cloves, crushed | 1 teaspoon finely grated fresh root ginger | ½ teaspoon turmeric | 625 g (1¼ lb) potatoes, cut into thick matchsticks and boiled | 150 ml (¼ pint) hot water | 1 courgette, cut into thick matchsticks and boiled | 2 plum tomatoes, finely chopped | ½ teaspoon garam masala | 4 tablespoons chopped coriander leaves | 2 tablespoons chopped mint leaves | juice and finely grated lime rind | salt

ONE Heat the oil in a large, nonstick wok or frying pan, add the onion and stir-fry for 5–6 minutes until softened. **TWO** Add the cumin seeds, garlic, ginger and turmeric. Stir-fry for 2–3 minutes, then add the potatoes with the water. Cook over a high heat for 3–4 minutes, and stir in the courgette, tomatoes and garam masala. Cook on high for 3–4 minutes, remove from the heat and stir in the herbs and the lime rind and juice. Season well.

Serves 4

NUTRIENT ANALYSIS PER SERVING 858 kJ – 204 kcal – 8 g protein – 36 g carbohydrate – 4 g sugars – 5 g fat – 1 g saturates – 6 g fibre – 20 mg sodium

GREEN BEAN STIR-FRY WITH CURRY LEAVES

Fresh crunchy beans, cooked in spices until barely tender, then sprinkled with freshly grated coconut, make a delicious accompaniment to simply cooked meat and fish dishes.

INGREDIENTS 1 tablespoon sunflower oil | 1 teaspoon black mustard seeds | 10–12 curry leaves | 1 teaspoon urad dhal | 1–2 dried red chillies | 1 small onion, halved and thinly sliced | 1 teaspoon turmeric | 400 g (13 oz) fine green beans, trimmed | 100 ml (3½ fl oz) water | salt | 2 tablespoons freshly grated coconut

ONE Heat the oil in a large, nonstick frying pan or wok. Add the mustard seeds and cook over a medium heat. As soon as the seeds start to 'pop', add the curry leaves, urad dhal and dried red chillies. Stir-fry for 1–2 minutes or until the dhal turns lightly golden. **TWO** Add the onion and stir and cook for 5–6 minutes until softened, then add the turmeric and continue to stir-fry for 2–3 minutes. **THREE** Add the beans to the pan with the measured water, stir, cover and cook over a medium-low heat for 5–6 minutes, stirring occasionally. Season well and remove from the heat. Sprinkle over the coconut just before serving.

Serves 4

NUTRIENT ANALYSIS PER SERVING 387 kJ – 93 kcal – 3 g protein – 7 g carbohydrate – 3 g sugars – 6 g fat – 2 g saturates – 4 g fibre – 4 mg sodium

HEALTHY TIP For maximum nutrition, buy beans in season and choose firm, crisp specimens and avoid pre-trimmed vegetables or any that are going soft.

MIXED VEGETABLE AND COCONUT STEW

INGREDIENTS 2 carrots, cut into thin batons | 1 courgette, cut into thin batons | 200 g (7 oz) green beans, trimmed and cut in half | 1 medium potato, cut into thin batons | 1 tablespoon sunflower oil | 1 large onion, halved and thinly sliced | ½ teaspoon black mustard seeds | 6–8 curry leaves | 1 green chilli, thinly sliced | 1 teaspoon poppy seeds | 200 ml (7 fl oz) coconut milk | juice of half a lemon | 150 ml (¼ pint) water | salt

ONE Place the vegetables in a bowl of cold water. **TWO** Heat the oil in a large, nonstick wok or frying pan and when it is hot add the onion. Cook over a medium heat for 4–5 minutes. Add the mustard seeds, curry leaves and green chilli and stir-fry for 2–3 minutes. **THREE** Drain the vegetables and add them to the pan with the poppy seeds, coconut milk, lemon juice and the measured water. Season and bring to the boil. Reduce the heat, cover and cook gently for 6–7 minutes or until the vegetables are just tender and serve.

Serves 4

NUTRIENT ANALYSIS PER SERVING 779 kJ – 188 kcal – 4 g protein – 17 g carbohydrate – 9 g sugars – 12 g fat – 6 g saturates – 4 g fibre – 70 mg sodium

CUCUMBER AND COCONUT CURRY

Mild-tasting cucumber is complemented perfectly by hot chillies, fragrant spices, tart tamarind and rich, sweet coconut in this utterly delectable stir-fry. Serve as a vegetable accompaniment with meat, fish or other vegetable dishes.

INGREDIENTS 1 tablespoon tamarind paste | 4 tablespoons water | ½ teaspoon fenugreek seeds | 2 dried red chillies | 100 g (3½ oz) freshly grated coconut | ½ teaspoon turmeric | 2 tablespoons sunflower oil | 1 tablespoon mustard seeds | 1 teaspoon cumin seeds | 8–10 curry leaves | 500 g (1 lb) cucumber, cut into 1 cm (½ inch) dice | salt

ONE Mix the tamarind paste with the measured water and set aside. **TWO** In a frying pan, dry-roast the fenugreek seeds and red chillies for 1 minute over a low heat. Transfer them to a mortar and pestle with the tamarind mixture, half the coconut and the turmeric and pound to a coarse paste. **THREE** Heat the oil in a frying pan and when hot add the mustard seeds. As soon as they start to 'pop', stir in the cumin seeds, curry leaves and the coconut mixture. Stir and cook over a medium heat for 2–3 minutes and then add the cucumber. Continue to stir and cook for 5–6 minutes, season well and sprinkle over the remaining coconut. Serve immediately.

Serves 4

NUTRIENT ANALYSIS PER SERVING 788 kJ – 190 kcal – 3 g protein – 8 g carbohydrate – 5 g sugars – 16 g fat – 8 g saturates – 4 g fibre – 12 mg sodium

HEALTHY TIP Cucumber may seem an unusual vegetable to stir-fry, but it tastes delicious and also has several health benefits. Cucumbers are a natural diuretic and are also believed to help reduce high blood pressure.

PEA AND POTATO BHAJI

INGREDIENTS 1 tablespoon light olive oil │ 2 teaspoons black mustard seeds │ 1 tablespoon fresh root ginger, peeled and cut into fine strips │ 2 teaspoons cumin seeds │ 2 dried red chillies │ 400 g (13 oz) fresh or frozen garden peas │ 400 g (13 oz) potatoes, boiled and cut into 1.5 cm (¾ inch) dice │ 2–3 tablespoons water │ sea salt │ 1 tablespoon freshly grated coconut, to garnish

ONE Heat the oil in a large nonstick frying pan and when it is hot add the mustard seeds. Stir-fry for 2–3 minutes until they start to 'pop', then add the ginger, cumin, red chilli, peas and potatoes. **TWO** Stir-fry over a high heat for 3–4 minutes, add the water, cover and reduce the heat to low. Cook gently for 2–3 minutes and remove from the heat. Season and sprinkle over the coconut and serve with rotis or flatbreads.

Serves 4

NUTRIENT ANALYSIS PER SERVING 940 kJ – 225 kcal – 11 g protein – 31 g carbohydrate – 3 g sugars – 7 g fat – 2 g saturates – 7 g fibre – 14 mg sodium

HEALTHY TIP Dishes rich in carbohydrate, such as this potato one, should be combined with fresh vegetables and a protein dish, such as a fish or meat curry or dhal.

BROCCOLI WITH GARLIC, CUMIN AND RED CHILLI

Crisp, fresh broccoli is delicious stir-fried with garlic, chilli and warm spices. The simple, clean flavours make this dish the perfect accompaniment to richer meat or fish dishes.

INGREDIENTS 1 tablespoon chickpea flour (besan or gram flour) | 1 teaspoon salt | 1 teaspoon ground cumin | 1 teaspoon ground coriander | ½ teaspoon garam masala | 2 tablespoons light olive oil | 4 garlic cloves, thinly sliced | 2 teaspoons cumin seeds | 2 red chillies, deseeded and sliced | 625 g (1¼ lb) broccoli florets | 1–2 tablespoons water

ONE In a small bowl mix together the chickpea flour, salt, ground cumin, ground coriander and garam masala. **TWO** Heat the oil in a large, nonstick wok or frying pan; when it is hot add the garlic, cumin seeds and chilli and stir-fry for 1–2 minutes. **THREE** Add the broccoli and stir-fry over a high heat for 3–4 minutes. Reduce the heat to low and evenly sprinkle the chickpea flour mixture over the broccoli. Cover the pan and cook gently for 5–6 minutes. **FOUR** Take the lid off the pan and sprinkle the measured water over the broccoli; stir and cook until the florets are evenly coated with the mixture. Check the seasoning and serve immediately.

Serves 4

NUTRIENT ANALYSIS PER SERVING 557 kJ – 134 kcal – 9 g protein – 7 g carbohydrate – 2 g sugars – 8 g fat – 1 g saturates – 1 g fibre – 505 mg sodium

HEALTHY TIP Broccoli is a good source of vitamin C, folic acid, iron and potassium and is also believed to have cancer-fighting properties. Cooking it lightly in this way, destroys fewer of its natural nutrients than boiling.

recipe illustrated on pages 132–133

TOMATO EGG CURRY

Whole boiled eggs cooked in a spiced sauce is a popular dish throughout India. Serve them with simple boiled rice or flatbreads and a vegetable accompaniment or salad for a healthy, nutritious meal.

INGREDIENTS 1 tablespoon sunflower oil │ 1 large onion, halved and thinly sliced │ 1 teaspoon finely grated fresh root ginger │ 2 garlic cloves, crushed │ 2 tablespoons medium curry powder │ 1 x 400 g (13 oz) can chopped tomatoes │ 1 teaspoon honey or sugar │ 8 large eggs, hard-boiled, peeled and halved │ salt │ 4 tablespoons low-fat yogurt, to drizzle over

TO GARNISH chopped coriander leaves │ roasted cumin seeds

ONE Heat the oil in a large, nonstick frying pan and add the onion. Cook over a medium heat for 10–12 minutes until softened and lightly golden. Add the ginger, garlic and curry powder and stir and cook for 1 minute. **TWO** Stir in the chopped tomatoes and sugar, bring the mixture to the boil, reduce the heat, cover and cook gently for 10–12 minutes, stirring often. Carefully add the eggs to the mixture and heat through gently until warmed. Drizzle over the yogurt, sprinkle over the coriander and cumin seeds, season and serve immediately with steamed rice or warmed flatbread.

Serves 4

NUTRIENT ANALYSIS PER SERVING 1252 kJ – 300 kcal – 21 g protein – 14 g carbohydrate – 11 g sugars – 18 g fat – 5 g saturates – 3 g fibre – 284 mg sodium

HEALTHY TIP Eggs are an excellent vegetarian source of protein, but they are also high in cholesterol, so anyone on a low-cholesterol diet should be careful not to eat too many eggs per week.

SPINACH, RED PEPPER AND CHICKPEA BHAJI

INGREDIENTS 1 tablespoon sunflower oil │ 1 teaspoon finely grated fresh root ginger │ 2 garlic cloves, crushed │ 1 large shallot, finely chopped │ 1 red pepper, deseeded and cut into thin strips │ 1 teaspoon chilli powder │ 1 teaspoon ground cumin │ 1 teaspoon ground coriander │ 2 tablespoons tomato purée │ 300 ml (½ pint) water │ 400 g (13 oz) baby spinach leaves │ 1 x 400 g (13 oz) can chickpeas, drained │ salt

ONE Heat the oil in a large nonstick frying pan. Add the ginger and garlic and stir-fry for 30 seconds. Add the shallot and red pepper and cook for 5–6 minutes until slightly softened.

TWO Stir in the chilli powder, ground cumin, ground coriander and tomato purée. Stir-fry for 2–3 minutes, then pour in the measured water, stir and bring to the boil. Stir in the spinach and chickpeas and cook for 5–6 minutes until the spinach has just wilted. Season.

Serves 4

NUTRIENT ANALYSIS PER SERVING 743 kJ – 177 kcal – 11 g protein – 21 g carbohydrate – 6 g sugars – 6 g fat – 1 g saturates – 9 g fibre – 185 mg sodium

MASALA GRILLED TOMATOES

These spicy tomatoes make a great accompaniment to meat and fish dishes, but they're also good served on toast as a satisfying snack.

INGREDIENTS 750 g (1½ lb) ripe, fresh plum tomatoes | 1 teaspoon garam masala | 1 teaspoon ground coriander | 2 teaspoons cumin seeds | ½ teaspoon chilli powder | juice of 1 lemon | light olive oil, to drizzle | salt and freshly ground black pepper | roughly chopped coriander and mint leaves, to garnish

ONE Cut the tomatoes in half, lengthways and lay them on a grill rack, cut side up. Sprinkle over the garam masala, ground coriander, cumin seeds, chilli powder and lemon juice. Lightly drizzle with the olive oil and season well. **TWO** Place under a preheated grill turned up high, about 10 cm (4 inches) from the source of the heat, and grill for 5–6 minutes or until the tops are lightly browned and the tomatoes slightly limp. Remove from the grill and place on a serving plate. Sprinkle over the chopped herbs and serve immediately.

Serves 4

NUTRIENT ANALYSIS PER SERVING 249 kJ – 59 kcal – 2 g protein – 7 g carbohydrate – 6 g sugars – 3 g fat – 1 g saturates – 3 g fibre – 27 g sodium

HEALTHY TIP Tomatoes contain the phytochemical lycopene, which is thought to protect against certain cancers. Cooked tomatoes are a richer source of lycopene than fresh.

INDIAN MASALA OMELETTE

Perfect for a lazy weekend breakfast or brunch, this hot and spicy omelette is a meal in itself. It's also great served with salad for a light lunch or supper.

INGREDIENTS 1 teaspoon sunflower oil │ ½ small red onion, very finely diced │ 1 plum tomato, deseeded and very finely diced │ 1 green chilli, deseeded and thinly sliced │ pinch of turmeric │ ½ teaspoon cumin seeds │ 2 tablespoons chopped coriander leaves │ 2 large eggs, lightly beaten │ ½ teaspoon salt

ONE Heat the oil in a medium-sized, nonstick frying pan. Mix together all the ingredients and pour into the pan. Cook over a medium heat for 3–4 minutes, or until the base of the omelette is lightly browned. With a spatula, carefully fold over the omelette, press it down lightly with a spatula and cook for 2–3 minutes. Then flip it over and cook for another 2–3 minutes or until it is cooked to your liking. **TWO** Remove from the heat and serve immediately with warm crusty bread or roll it up in a warm chapatti.

Serves 1

NUTRIENT ANALYSIS PER SERVING 972 kJ – 234 kcal – 16 g protein – 6 g carbohydrate – 4 g sugars – 16 g fat – 4 g saturates – 1 g fibre – 175 mg sodium

HEALTHY TIP Hot chillies are thought to boost the immune system and are often recommended for warding off colds and fevers.

PUMPKIN CURRY

On cooking, pumpkin becomes sweet and makes the perfect partner for fiery chilli and warm spices such as cumin and turmeric. Despite its quick cooking time, this dish has a rounded flavour.

INGREDIENTS 500 g (1 lb) pumpkin or butternut squash, cut into 2.5 cm (1 inch) cubes | 1 teaspoon turmeric | 1 teaspoon smoked paprika | 750 ml (1¼ pints) water | 200 g (7 oz) freshly grated coconut | 1 teaspoon cumin seeds | 1 tablespoon sunflower oil | 1 teaspoon black mustard seeds | 8–10 curry leaves | 2 small red chillies, split in half lengthways | salt

ONE Put the pumpkin or butternut squash in a saucepan with the turmeric, smoked paprika and the measured water. Bring to the boil and simmer gently for 6–8 minutes or until tender. **TWO** Grind half of the coconut in a spice mill or a mortar and pestle with the cumin seeds. Stir this into the pumpkin mixture and cook for 2–3 minutes. Remove from the heat. **THREE** In a small, nonstick frying pan, heat the oil until hot and add the mustard seeds, curry leaves and red chillies. Stir and cook over a high heat for 1–2 minutes, then tip this mixture over the pumpkin curry. Season and serve.

Serves 4

NUTRIENT ANALYSIS PER SERVING 976 kJ – 236 kcal – 3 g protein – 7 g carbohydrate – 4 g sugars – 22 g fat – 16 g saturates – 7 g fibre – 12 mg sodium

HEALTHY TIP Orange-fleshed vegetables, such as squashes, are an excellent source of the immune-boosting nutrient betacarotene, also said to help protect against heart disease .

MUSTARD BRAISED SPICED CABBAGE

Mustard seeds, cooked in hot oil until they 'pop', have a sweet, nutty taste and are a classic flavouring for many Indian vegetable dishes. They work well here combined with lightly cooked, sweet and tender cabbage.

INGREDIENTS 1 tablespoon sunflower oil │ 1½ tablespoons black mustard seeds │ 10–12 fresh curry leaves │ 1 teaspoon dried urad dhal │ 2 onions, halved and very thinly sliced │ 2 dried red chillies │ 1 teaspoon turmeric │ 500 g (1 lb) green or white cabbage, very finely shredded │ 100 ml (3½ fl oz) water │ salt │ freshly grated coconut, to garnish

ONE Heat the oil in a large, nonstick frying pan over a medium heat. Add the mustard seeds and when they start to 'pop' add the curry leaves and urad dhal. Stir-fry for 2–3 minutes or until the dhal starts to brown. **TWO** Stir in the onions and red chillies. Cook over a high heat, stirring often, for 4–5 minutes or until the onions soften. Add the turmeric and the cabbage and stir and cook for 2–3 minutes. Add the measured water, cover and cook gently for 5–7 minutes or until the cabbage has softened, but still retains a bite. Season and serve immediately, sprinkled with freshly grated coconut.

Serves 4

NUTRIENT ANALYSIS PER SERVING 616 kJ – 148 kcal – 6 g protein – 15 g carbohydrate – 9 g sugars – 7 g fat – 2 g saturates – 6 g fibre – 14 mg sodium

HEALTHY TIP Cabbage is a member of the brassica family, which contains a rich supply of health-giving nutrients, including those that are believed to help protect against cancer. Green cabbage has more potent health-giving properties than white, but white cabbage gives particularly delicious sweet, crisp results.

recipe illustrated on pages 144–145

CAULIFLOWER TARKA

Tarka is a seasoning technique unique to India. Spices are cooked in very hot oil, to release their flavour, then the oil is used to season the food. Here, cauliflower is cooked in the flavoured oil until just tender, to make a delicious vegetable dish.

INGREDIENTS 1 tablespoon sunflower oil | 1 teaspoon cumin seeds | 1 teaspoon yellow mustard seeds | 500 g (1 lb) cauliflower florets | 2 garlic cloves, finely chopped | 2.5 cm (1 inch) piece of fresh root ginger, cut into fine shreds | 2 red chillies, sliced | ½ teaspoon garam masala | 200 ml (7 fl oz) hot water | salt and freshly ground black pepper

ONE Heat the oil in a large nonstick wok or frying pan over a medium heat. Add the cumin and mustard seeds. Stir-fry for 1 minute, then add the cauliflower, garlic, ginger and red chillies. **TWO** Turn the heat to high and stir-fry for 6–7 minutes until the cauliflower is lightly browned at the edges. Stir in the garam masala along with the measured water, stir to mix well, cover and cook on high for 1–2 minutes. Remove from the heat, season and serve immediately.

Serves 4

NUTRIENT ANALYSIS PER SERVING 359 kJ – 86 kcal – 6 g protein – 6 g carbohydrate – 3 g sugars – 5 g fat – 1 g saturates – 2 g fibre – 15 mg sodium

HEALTHY TIP Cauliflower is a member of the brassica family which contains valuable phytochemicals and it is believed that these help prevent and fight against cancer.

GRAINS, RI
AND BREAD

ES, PULSES
S

SPICED LEMON RICE

A typical southern Indian favourite, this citrus-flavoured rice dish is a perfect accompaniment to plain grilled fish or chicken.

INGREDIENTS 200 g (7 oz) basmati rice | 1 tablespoon light olive oil | 12–14 fresh curry leaves | 1 dried red chilli | 2.5 cm (1 inch) piece of cassia bark or cinnamon stick | 2 or 3 cloves | 4–6 cardamom pods | 2 teaspoons cumin seeds | ¼ teaspoon turmeric | juice of 1 large lemon | 450 ml (¾ pint) boiling water | sea salt

ONE Place the rice in a sieve and wash it thoroughly under cold running water. Drain well and set aside. **TWO** Heat the oil in a nonstick saucepan; when it is hot add the curry leaves, chilli, cassia or cinnamon, cloves, cardamom, cumin seeds and turmeric. Stir-fry for 20–30 seconds and add the rice. Stir-fry for 2 minutes, then add the lemon juice and the measured water. Bring to the boil, cover the pan tightly and reduce the heat to low. **THREE** Cook for 10–12 minutes, remove from the heat and allow to stand undisturbed for 10 minutes. Fluff up the rice with a fork and season before serving.

Serves 4

NUTRIENT ANALYSIS PER SERVING 1009 kJ – 240 kcal – 5 g protein – 46 g carbohydrate – 0 g sugars – 4 g fat – 1 g saturates – 0 g fibre – 4 mg sodium

HEALTHY TIP Lemons are an excellent source of vitamin C, which is important for boosting the immune system, healing wounds and protecting against heart disease. Vitamin C also helps the body absorb iron.

BRINJAL AND CASHEW NUT RICE

Brinjal is the Indian name for aubergine, which is enjoyed in a great many ways in Indian cooking. Here, the chunks of moist, juicy aubergine are in perfect contrast with the fluffy rice and rich, tender cashew nuts.

INGREDIENTS 300 g (10 oz) basmati rice | 2 tablespoons sunflower oil | 4 shallots, thinly sliced | 1 teaspoon black mustard seeds | 2 dried red chillies | 6–8 curry leaves | 2.5 cm (1 inch) piece of cassia bark or cinnamon stick | 2–3 cardamom pods | 1 bay leaf | 200 g (7 oz) aubergine, cut into bite-sized cubes | 1 teaspoon turmeric | 600 ml (1 pint) boiling water | salt

TO SERVE juice of ½ lemon | 200 g (8 oz) roasted red pepper, diced | 50 g (2 oz) roasted cashew nuts | chopped coriander leaves

ONE Wash the rice in several changes of cold water, drain and set aside. **TWO** Heat the oil in a large, nonstick wok or frying pan and when it is hot add the shallots, mustard seeds, dried red chillies, curry leaves, cassia or cinnamon, cardamom and bay leaf. Stir and fry for 1–2 minutes, then add the drained rice. Stir gently to coat the rice with the spice mixture, then add the aubergine and turmeric. Stir to mix well and pour in the measured water. Season well and bring to the boil. Cover tightly, reduce the heat to low and cook gently for 12–15 minutes. Remove from the heat and allow to stand, covered and undisturbed for another 10 minutes. Squeeze over the lemon juice, add the pepper, fluff up the grains of rice with a fork and sprinkle over the cashew nuts and fresh coriander. Serve immediately.

Serves 4

NUTRIENT ANALYSIS PER SERVING 1778 kJ – 426 kcal – 9 g protein – 67 g carbohydrate – 3 g sugars – 12 g fat – 1 g saturates – 2 g fibre – 6 mg sodium

HEALTHY TIP Cashew nuts not only add texture and flavour to this dish, but also provide protein and are a good source of the B vitamins.

recipe illustrated on pages 156–157

YOGURT AND HERB RICE

Lightly spiced rice, tossed with fresh herbs and yogurt, makes a tasty alternative to plain boiled or steamed rice. Yogurt is naturally cooling, so this dish makes a great accompaniment to really hot and spicy curries.

INGREDIENTS 625 g (1¼ lb) basmati rice │ 1 tablespoon sunflower oil │ 1 teaspoon cumin seeds │ ½ teaspoon crushed coriander seeds │ 1 teaspoon black mustard seeds │ 1 red chilli │ ½ teaspoon grated fresh root ginger │ 750 g (1½ lb) very low-fat natural yogurt │ 8 tablespoons chopped fresh dill │ salt │ chopped red chillies, to garnish

ONE Cook the rice according to the packet instructions until just tender, drain and set aside.

TWO Heat the oil in a large, nonstick frying pan and when it is hot add the cumin seeds, coriander seeds and mustard seeds. As the seeds begin to 'pop', add the chilli and ginger, stir-fry for a few seconds and then pour this mixture over the rice and stir to mix evenly.

THREE Whisk the yogurt until smooth and stir it into the spiced rice with the chopped dill. Season and serve immediately with chopped red chillies to garnish.

Serves 4

NUTRIENT ANALYSIS PER SERVING 2898 kJ – 692 kcal – 22 g protein – 136 g carbohydrate – 15 g sugars – 6 g fat – 1 g saturates – 0 g fibre – 170 g sodium

MINTED RICE WITH TOMATO AND SPROUTED BEANS

INGREDIENTS 2 tablespoons light olive oil │ 6 spring onions, very finely sliced │ 2 garlic cloves, finely chopped │ 750 g (1½ lb) cooked, cooled Basmati rice │ 2 ripe plum tomatoes, finely chopped │ 250 g (8 oz) mixed sprouted beans (a mixture of aduki, mung, lentil, chickpea sprouts) │ a small handful of mint leaves │ salt and freshly ground black pepper

ONE Heat the oil in a large, nonstick wok or frying pan. When it is hot, add the spring onions and garlic and stir-fry for 2–3 minutes. **TWO** Add the cooked rice and continue to stir-fry over a high heat for 3–4 minutes. Stir in the tomatoes and mixed sprouted beans and continue to cook over a high heat for 2–3 minutes or until warmed through. **THREE** Remove from the heat, season and stir in the chopped mint leaves. Serve immediately.

Serves 4

NUTRIENT ANALYSIS PER SERVING 1250 kJ – 296 kcal – 6 g protein – 56 g carbohydrate – 3 g sugars – 7 g fat – 1 g saturates – 6 g fibre – 12 mg sodium

SPICED VEGETABLE SEMOLINA

This hearty dish, known as *uppama*, is rather like a pilaf. It comes from the south-western state of Kerala, where there are many variations using different combinations of spices and vegetables. Mustard seeds are a traditional flavouring.

INGREDIENTS 175 g (6 oz) coarse semolina │ 1 tablespoon sunflower oil │ 1 teaspoon black mustard seeds │ 1 teaspoon cumin seeds │ 1 dried red chilli │ 10–12 curry leaves │ 1 onion, finely chopped │ 1 teaspoon garam masala │ 1 carrot, finely diced │ 100 g (3½ oz) fresh peas │ 10–12 cherry tomatoes, halved │ 600 ml (1 pint) boiling water │ salt │ freshly chopped coriander leaves, to garnish │ lemon wedges, to serve

ONE Place the semolina in a large, nonstick frying pan and dry-roast it over a medium heat for 8–10 minutes or until golden brown. Remove from the pan and set aside. **TWO** Return the pan to the heat and add the oil. When it is hot, add the mustard seeds, cumin seeds, chilli, curry leaves and onion. Stir-fry over a medium heat for 5–6 minutes or until the onion has softened, then add the garam masala, carrot, peas and cherry tomatoes. Stir-fry for 1–2 minutes, add the semolina and the measured water. Stir and cook for 5–6 minutes over a low heat, until the semolina has absorbed all the water. Season, and garnish with chopped coriander before serving with wedges of lemon to squeeze over.

Serves 4

NUTRIENT ANALYSIS PER SERVING 1024 kJ – 243 kcal – 8 g protein – 44 g carbohydrate – 6 g sugars – 5 g fat – 1 g saturates – 4 g fibre – 19 mg sodium

HEALTHY TIP Starchy carbohydrates, such as the semolina used here, should form a part of every meal. They provide the body with energy, to help keep you going throughout the day.

recipe illustrated on pages 164–165

CHICKEN AND MUSHROOM PULAO

Tasty and sustaining, this richly flavoured rice dish can be served as a meal in itself, or with a light and crunchy salad and, perhaps, some Date, Apricot and Raisin Chutney (see page 206).

INGREDIENTS 1 tablespoon sunflower oil │ 1 onion, finely diced │ 1 teaspoon finely grated fresh root ginger │ 1 teaspoon finely grated garlic │ 2 teaspoons ground cumin │ ½ teaspoon crushed cardamom seeds │ 2.5 cm (1 inch) piece of cassia bark or cinnamon stick │ 4 cloves │ 250 g (8 oz) skinless, boneless chicken thighs, cut into bite-sized pieces │ 200 g (7 oz) shiitake mushrooms, thickly sliced │ 100 g (3½ oz) green beans, cut into 2.5 cm (1 inch) lengths │ 600 ml (1 pint) fresh chicken stock │ 300 g (10 oz) basmati rice, washed and drained │ salt and freshly ground black pepper

ONE Heat the oil in a large, heavy-based frying pan and add the onion. Cook over a medium heat for 10–12 minutes or until it is softened and lightly browned. Add the ginger, garlic, cumin, cardamom, cassia bark or cinnamon stick and cloves. Stir-fry for 2–3 minutes, then add the chicken and cook over a high heat for 5–6 minutes. **TWO** Stir in the mushrooms, green beans, stock and rice, season and bring to the boil. Cover tightly, turn the heat to low and cook gently for 12–15 minutes. Remove from the heat and allow to stand undisturbed and uncovered for another 10 minutes. Fluff up the grains of the rice with a fork and serve warm.

Serves 4

NUTRIENT ANALYSIS PER SERVING 1685 kJ – 403 kcal – 20 g protein – 63 g carbohydrate – 2 g sugars – 8 g fat – 2 g saturates – 2 g fibre – 306 mg sodium

HEALTHY TIP A classic pulao often uses a generous quantity of oil, but this modern version uses only a little oil to fry the spices and aromatics and release their flavours. Using skinless chicken will further reduce the fat content of the dish.

CHICKPEA CURRY

Chickpeas are an ancient food, eaten for millennia and are a popular ingredient in Indian cooking. This classic curry uses canned chickpeas, so it takes virtually no time to cook and is perfect served as a vegetarian main dish or as one of several vegetable dishes.

INGREDIENTS 1 tablespoon sunflower oil | 2 garlic cloves, crushed | 1 teaspoon finely grated fresh root ginger | 2 tablespoons medium or hot curry powder | 1 x 400 g (13 oz) can chopped tomatoes | 1 teaspoon grated jaggery or palm sugar | 2 x 400 g (13 oz) cans chickpeas, rinsed and drained | salt | low-fat yogurt, to drizzle | small handful of chopped coriander leaves, to garnish

ONE Heat the oil in a large, nonstick wok or frying pan and add the garlic and ginger. Stir-fry for 30 seconds and add the curry powder. Stir and cook for 1 minute before adding the chopped tomatoes and jaggery or palm sugar. Bring the mixture to the boil, cover, reduce the heat and cook on a medium heat for 10–12 minutes. **TWO** Stir in the chickpeas and mix well. Cook over a medium heat for 3–4 minutes. Season, remove from the heat. Drizzle with the low-fat yogurt and sprinkle over the chopped coriander before serving.

Serves 4

NUTRIENT ANALYSIS PER SERVING 1232 kJ – 292 kcal – 16 g protein – 39 g carbohydrate – 5 g sugars – 9 g fat – 1 g saturates – 1 g fibre – 503 mg sodium

HEALTHY TIP Pulses, such as chickpeas, contain useful amounts of various nutrients, including B vitamins, iron, calcium and fibre. They are also a good source of complex carbohydrates, which are absorbed slowly into the body, providing a steady stream of energy to be released.

recipe illustrated on pages 170–171

MINTED GREEN MUNG BEAN CURRY

INGREDIENTS 250 g (8 oz) green mung beans │ 1 teaspoon chilli powder │ ½ teaspoon turmeric │ 750 ml (1¼ pints) water │ 2 potatoes, diced │ 150 ml (¼ pint) half-fat coconut milk │ 2 plum tomatoes, roughly chopped │ 1 green chilli, deseeded and finely chopped │ 1–2 teaspoons grated palm sugar │ small handful roughly chopped mint leaves and coriander leaves │ salt

ONE Place the mung beans, chilli powder and turmeric in a large saucepan with the measured water. Bring to the boil, cover, reduce the heat and cook gently for 20–25 minutes. Add the potatoes and continue to cook for 12–15 minutes or until tender. **TWO** Stir in the coconut milk, tomatoes and green chilli and cook gently for 4–5 minutes. Stir in the palm sugar and cook for 2–3 minutes until dissolved. **THREE** Remove from the heat, stir in the chopped herbs, season and serve immediately.

Serves 4

NUTRIENT ANALYSIS PER SERVING 1180 kJ – 278 kcal – 17 g protein – 46 g carbohydrate – 7 g sugars – 4 g fat – 2 g saturates – 10 g fibre – 68 mg sodium

HEALTHY TIP Pale green mung beans are an excellent source of protein and they also offer a valuable source of fibre, which is essential for good digestion.

SPINACH DHAL

No Indian meal is complete without a bowl of spicy lentil dhal – one of the staple dishes eaten throughout the country. This version is flecked with fresh, tender baby spinach for extra flavour, colour and texture.

INGREDIENTS 250 g (8 oz) red lentils, rinsed and drained │ 1.2 litres (2 pints) water │ ¼ teaspoon turmeric │ 1 teaspoon finely grated fresh root ginger │ 100 g (3½ oz) baby spinach leaves, chopped │ large handful of fresh coriander leaves, chopped │ 2 teaspoons light olive oil │ 5 garlic cloves, finely sliced │ 2 teaspoons cumin seeds │ 2 teaspoons mustard seeds │ 1 tablespoon ground cumin │ 1 teaspoon ground coriander │ 1 red chilli, finely chopped │ sea salt

ONE Place the lentils in a large saucepan with the water, turmeric and ginger. Bring to the boil. Skim off any scum that forms on the surface. **TWO** Lower the heat and cook gently for 20 minutes, stirring occasionally. Add the spinach and chopped coriander, stir and cook for 8–10 minutes. **THREE** Heat the oil in a small, nonstick frying pan and when it is hot add the garlic, cumin and mustard seeds, ground cumin, ground coriander and red chilli. Stir-fry over a high heat for 2–3 minutes, then tip this mixture into the lentils. Stir to mix well, season and serve immediately with rice or naan bread.

Serves 4

NUTRIENT ANALYSIS PER SERVING 1050 kJ – 248 kcal – 17 g protein – 38 g carbohydrate – 2 g sugars – 4 g fat – 0 g saturates – 8 g fibre – 65 mg sodium

HEALTHY TIP Both lentils and spinach are an excellent source of iron, making this dish a real iron-booster. Lentils are also a great source of fibre and protein, so dhal is a perfect choice for a vegetarian meal.

recipe illustrated on pages 176–177

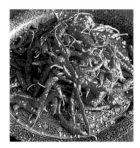

HERBED BEAN AND NEW POTATO SALAD

This refreshing, wholesome salad is the perfect accompaniment to grilled, spicy fish or meat dishes. The yogurt dressing is cooling too, so if you're not used to hot food, it's the perfect choice.

INGREDIENTS 8–10 small baby new potatoes │ 1 garlic clove, crushed │ ½ teaspoon ground cumin │ ½ teaspoon ground coriander │ ½ teaspoon crushed dried red chillies │ 1 teaspoon golden caster sugar │ 100 g (3½ oz) very low-fat natural yogurt │ 100 g (3½ oz) very low-fat natural fromage frais │ juice of 1 lime │ 2 spring onions, finely chopped │ ½ red pepper, very finely diced │ 100 g (3½ oz) each canned red kidney beans and black-eyed beans, rinsed and drained │ a small handful each of roughly chopped coriander and mint leaves │ salt

ONE Boil the potatoes until tender and halve them. Place them in a large mixing bowl and set aside. **TWO** Whisk together the garlic, cumin, coriander, dried chilli, sugar, yogurt, fromage frais and lime juice. Add this to the potatoes with the spring onion, red pepper and beans. Season well and add the chopped herbs. Toss to mix well before serving.

Serves 4

NUTRIENT ANALYSIS PER SERVING 526 kJ – 124 kcal – 8 g protein – 22 g carbohydrate – 8 g sugars – 1 g fat – 0 g saturates – 3 g fibre – 139 mg sodium

HEALTHY TIP The good intentions of a healthy salad can often be ruined by the addition of a rich, creamy dressing – but this low-fat yogurt-based dressing is just the thing for health-conscious eating.

CORIANDER AND CUMIN-FLECKED ROTI

INGREDIENTS 400 g (13 oz) plain wholemeal flour, plus extra for dusting │ 1 teaspoon salt │ 3–4 teaspoons cumin seeds │ 2 tablespoons very finely chopped coriander leaves │ 2–3 tablespoons light olive oil │ 250 ml (8 fl oz) lukewarm water

ONE Mix together the flour, salt, cumin and coriander in a large mixing bowl. Add the oil and work it into the mixture with your fingers. Gradually add the measured water and knead for 5–6 minutes until smooth, adding a little extra flour if necessary. Cover the dough with a damp cloth and allow it to rest for 30 minutes. **TWO** Divide the dough into 16 portions and form each into a round ball. Roll each ball into a 12–15 cm (5–6 inch) disc, lightly dusting with flour if required. **THREE** Heat a large cast-iron griddle pan or a heavy-based frying pan on a high heat. Cook the rotis, one at a time, for 45 seconds on one side, then flip over and continue to cook for 1–2 minutes until lightly browned at the edges. Remove and keep warm in foil as you cook the rest. Serve warm with a variety of dishes.

Makes 16

NUTRIENT ANALYSIS PER ROTI 416 kJ – 98 kcal – 3 g protein – 16 g carbohydrate – 1 g sugars – 3 g fat – 0 g saturates – 2 g fibre – 123 mg sodium

RED ONION, CHILLI AND GRAM FLOUR BREAD

Gram flour, or besan, is made from ground chickpeas and can be found in large supermarkets and Asian stores. It gives these tasty, spiced flatbreads a lovely nutty flavour.

INGREDIENTS 150 g (3½ oz) plain wholemeal flour │ 150 g (3½ oz) gram flour │ 1 red onion, finely diced │ 1 red chilli, deseeded and finely chopped │ 1 tablespoon chopped fresh coriander leaves │ 1 teaspoon cumin seeds │ 1 teaspoon black onion seeds (nigella) │ 100–150 ml (3½–5 fl oz) lukewarm water │ salt │ sunflower or light olive oil, for brushing

ONE Sift both the flours into a large mixing bowl and add the onion, red chilli, chopped coriander and cumin and onion seeds. Season and mix together. Gradually pour in the measured water and knead for 2–3 minutes on a lightly floured surface, to make a soft dough. Allow to rest for 5 minutes and then divide the dough into 8 portions. Shape each one into a ball. **TWO** Roll the balls out on a lightly floured surface to a 12 cm (5 inch) diameter disc. **THREE** Heat a large, flat griddle pan or nonstick frying pan until it is hot. Cook the rolled-out discs of dough, one at a time, for 30 seconds on one side; brush with a little oil, flip over and cook for 1 minute, moving the bread around. Then flip the dough over again to cook on the other side for 1 minute or until the bread is lightly browned on both sides. Remove and keep warm, wrapped in foil while you cook the remainder. Serve warm.

Makes 8

NUTRIENT ANALYSIS PER BREAD 412 kJ – 97 kcal – 5 g protein – 16 g carbohydrate – 1 g sugars – 2 g fat – 0 g saturates – 3 g fibre – 7 mg sodium

HEALTHY TIP To ensure that you use the minimum amount of oil, use a pastry brush or a piece of kitchen paper moistened with oil to prevent the breads sticking to the pan.

recipe illustrated on pages 184–185

DOSAS WITH PRAWNS AND CRAYFISH

These crispy, light pancakes, rolled around a hearty spiced filling, are an essential part of southern Indian dining. They're filling, though, so can be enjoyed as a meal in themselves, served simply with Coriander, Coconut and Mint Chutney *(see page 207)* and perhaps a fresh, crunchy salad.

INGREDIENTS FOR THE DOSAS 400 g (13 oz) rice flour │ ¼ teaspoon baking powder │ 1 egg │ 1 tablespoon sunflower oil │ ½ teaspoon finely crushed fenugreek seeds │ salt │ sunflower oil, for brushing

STUFFING 1 tablespoon sunflower oil │ 1 teaspoon cumin seeds │ 1 onion, halved and thinly sliced │ 2 teaspoons finely grated fresh root ginger │ 2 teaspoons finely grated garlic │ 1 red chilli, finely sliced │ 400 g (13 oz) cooked peeled prawns and crayfish tails │ 3 tablespoons chopped coriander and mint leaves │ salt

ONE Make the batter for the dosas by putting the rice flour, baking powder, egg, sunflower oil and fenugreek in a mixing bowl. Pour in cold water, slowly, whisking all the time to give you a batter that is the consistency of double cream. Season, cover and chill for 3–4 hours. **TWO** Meanwhile, make the filling. Heat the oil in a large frying pan and when it is hot add the cumin and onion. Cook over a gentle heat for 10–12 minutes or until the onion has softened, then add the ginger, garlic and red chilli. Stir and fry for 1–2 minutes before adding the prawns and crayfish. Stir and cook for 2–3 minutes, stir in the coriander, season and remove from the heat. Set aside and keep warm. **THREE** To make the dosas, brush a medium-sized nonstick frying pan with the oil and set it over a medium-high heat. Add a ladleful of the batter and swirl to cover the base of the pan evenly. Cook for 1–2 minutes, then flip and cook on the other side for 30 seconds. Repeat until all the batter has been used. Spoon over the prawn mixture and serve warm.

Serves 4

NUTRIENT ANALYSIS PER SERVING 750 kJ – 179 kcal – 10 g protein – 28 g carbohydrate – 1 g sugars – 2 g fat – 0 g saturates – 0 g fibre – 533 g sodium

HEALTHY TIP Fresh ginger, an essential spice in many Indian dishes, is great for stimulating the circulation.

recipe illustrated on pages 188–189

SPICED COURGETTE PANCAKES

These tasty little pancakes can be made in advance and warmed through in a low oven just before serving – perfect for entertaining. Fresh, tangy raita makes a lovely contrast to the rich, melting taste of the pancakes.

INGREDIENTS 150 g (5 oz) courgette, coarsely grated | 150 g (5 oz) desiccated coconut | 150 g (5 oz) gram flour | 1 teaspoon cumin seeds | 1 red chilli, finely chopped | 2 tablespoons finely chopped coriander leaves | salt | sunflower oil to grease the frying pan

MINT RAITA 8 tablespoons finely chopped mint leaves | 6 tablespoons low-fat natural yogurt | 1 teaspoon caster sugar | salt and freshly ground black pepper

ONE Squeeze out and discard all the liquid from the courgette and put the vegetable in a mixing bowl with the coconut, gram flour, cumin seeds, chilli and coriander. **TWO** Add a little water to blend until you have a batter of dropping consistency. Season. **THREE** Lightly grease a nonstick frying pan with the oil and set it over a medium heat. Ladle a spoonful of the batter into the pan and flatten it with the back of a spoon into a 10 cm (6 inch) disc. Cook for 2–3 minutes and then flip the pancake over and cook for 2–3 minutes until lightly browned. Remove from the pan, transfer to a plate and while you use up the rest of the batter, keep the cooked pancakes, covered, in a low oven until you are ready to serve. **FOUR** To make the raita, place all the ingredients in a food processor and blend until fairly smooth. Serve the courgette pancakes with the mint raita.

Serves 4

NUTRIENT ANALYSIS PER SERVING 1688 kJ – 405 kcal – 15 g protein – 29 g carbohydrate – 9 g sugars – 26 g fat – 20 g saturates – 15 g fibre – 79 mg sodium

HEALTHY TIP These golden vegetable pancakes make a terrific alternative to crunchy deep-fried poppadums that are often served before an Indian meal in the West. They're quite filling, though, so don't eat too many.

recipe illustrated on pages 192–193

RELISHES A
CHUTNEYS

ND

CUCUMBER AND MINT RAITA

Cool, fresh and versatile, this raita can be served as an accompaniment to almost any dish, snack or meal. The cool cucumber and yogurt mixture acts as a perfect foil, especially for spicy food.

INGREDIENTS 1 large cucumber, peeled | 250 ml (8 fl oz) very low-fat yogurt | 1 teaspoon caster sugar | 1 red chilli, deseeded and finely sliced | large handful of chopped mint leaves | juice of ½ lime | roasted cumin seeds and chilli powder, to sprinkle

ONE Halve the cucumber lengthways. Using a teaspoon, scoop out the seeds and discard. Either very finely slice or dice the cucumber and place it in a bowl. **TWO** Whisk the yogurt and sugar until smooth and add the chilli, mint leaves and lime juice. Season, pour over the cucumber and toss to mix well. Chill until ready to serve. Sprinkle with the cumin seeds and chilli powder just before serving.

Makes about 400 ml (14 fl oz)

NUTRIENT ANALYSIS PER TABLESPOON SERVING 220 kJ – 53 kcal – 4 g protein – 7 g carbohydrate – 7 g sugars – 1 g fat – 0 g saturates – 0 g fibre – 55 mg sodium

HEALTHY TIP Cucumber has a high water content and is very low in calories, making it the perfect food for anyone on a diet. Raw cucumbers can be hard to digest, but here the seeds are removed making them easier to stomach.

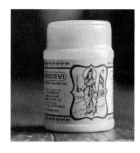

QUICK LEMON PICKLE

This quick pickle is made on the day you intend to use it, but it can be stored in an airtight jar or container in the fridge for 3–4 days. It makes a perfect accompaniment to any rice, lentil and vegetable dish.

INGREDIENTS 1 tablespoon sunflower oil | 1 teaspoon black mustard seeds | 6–8 curry leaves | 2 dried red chillies, roughly crushed | 2 tablespoons white wine vinegar | 300 g (10 oz) preserved or pickled lemons, roughly chopped | pinch of ground asafoetida | sea salt

ONE Heat the oil in a nonstick frying pan and when it is hot, add the mustard seeds. When they start to 'pop', add the curry leaves and dried red chillies. Remove from the heat and add the vinegar and the chopped lemon. **TWO** Return the pan to the heat and cook over a medium heat for 3–4 minutes. Add the asafoetida, season well and remove from the heat. Allow to cool completely before serving.

Makes about 350 ml (12 fl oz)

NUTRIENT ANALYSIS PER TABLESPOON SERVING 211 kJ – 50 kcal – 1 g protein – 3 g carbohydrate – 1 g sugars – 3 g fat – 0 g saturates – 1 g fibre – 6 mg sodium

HEALTHY TIP Traditional lemon pickle is very salty, but this light, fresh version uses less salt, so is better for your health. It won't keep as well, but it's so simple to make that it's worth making it fresh.

recipe illustrated on pages 202–203

TAMARIND AND RED PEPPER CHUTNEY

This delicious spicy chutney can be used as an accompaniment to many starters and snacks. I use it to give an ordinary cheese and ham sandwich a special extra 'kick'.

INGREDIENTS 100 g (3½ oz) block of tamarind │ 400 ml (14 fl oz) hot water │ 80 g (3 oz) grated jaggery or palm sugar │ 50 g (2 oz) soft brown sugar │ ½ red pepper, finely diced │ 6–8 black peppercorns │ 1 teaspoon red chilli powder │ 1 teaspoon sea salt │ 2 teaspoons cumin seeds │ 1 teaspoon ground cumin │ ½ teaspoon garam masala

ONE Place the block of tamarind in a saucepan with the measured water and bring to the boil. Reduce the heat and cook gently for 20 minutes until the tamarind has broken down and become pulpy. Remove from the heat and strain into a saucepan through a fine metal sieve, pressing down to extract as much liquid as possible. **TWO** Add the jaggery, soft brown sugar, red pepper, black peppercorns, chilli powder, salt, cumin seeds, ground cumin and garam masala to the tamarind liquid. Cook over a low heat for 15–20 minutes, stirring often. Remove from the heat and allow to cool before pouring it into a sterilized jar. This chutney will keep up to two weeks if stored in the refrigerator.

Makes 250 g (8 oz)

NUTRIENT ANALYSIS PER TABLESPOON SERVING 349 kJ – 82 kcal – 1 g protein – 20 g carbohydrate – 19 g sugars – 0.3 g fat – 0 g saturates – 0 g fibre – 206 mg sodium

HEALTHY TIP Red peppers are an excellent source of vitamin C and the immune-boosting antioxidant betacarotene.

DATE, APRICOT AND RAISIN CHUTNEY

This flavour-packed sweet and spicy chutney will liven up any dish you serve it with. The chutney can be stored in the fridge for up to 1 week.

INGREDIENTS 200 g (7 oz) ready-to-eat dried dates, stoned | 100 g (3½ oz) ready-to-eat dried apricots, stoned | 1 tablespoon tamarind paste | 3 tablespoons organic tomato ketchup | 1 teaspoon ground coriander | 2 teaspoons golden caster sugar | 1 teaspoon hot chilli powder | 1 tablespoon chopped mint leaves | 250 ml (8 fl oz) water | 50 g (2 oz) raisins or golden sultanas | salt

ONE Finely chop the dates and apricots and place them in a food processor with the tamarind paste, ketchup, ground coriander, sugar, chilli powder and mint leaves. **TWO** Add the measured water and pulse the mixture in the processor until combined but still slightly chunky. Scrape the mixture down the sides of the processor and pulse again for 1–2 minutes. **THREE** Transfer the date mixture to a bowl and stir in the raisins. Season, cover and chill until ready to serve.

Makes about 400 g (13 oz)

NUTRIENT ANALYSIS PER TABLESPOON SERVING 240 kJ – 56 kcal – 1 g protein – 14 g carbohydrate – 14 g sugars – 0.25 g fat – 0 g saturates – 2 g fibre – 67 mg sodium

CORIANDER, COCONUT AND MINT CHUTNEY

This fresh, spiced chutney can be served with snacks, as a dipping sauce or as a relish to spoon over grilled and barbecued fish and meat dishes. It will keep in the refrigerator for up to 1 week.

INGREDIENTS 200 g (7 oz) chopped coriander leaves │ 100 g (3½ oz) chopped mint leaves │ 50 g (2 oz) freshly grated coconut │ 1 teaspoon finely grated fresh root ginger │ 2 garlic cloves, crushed │ 4–6 green chillies (deseeded), chopped │ 2 tablespoons ground cashew nuts │ 1 teaspoon amchoor, or dried mango powder │ juice of ½ lemon │ 1–2 teaspoons golden caster sugar │ 150 ml (¼ pint) very low-fat natural yogurt │ salt

ONE Place all the ingredients in a food processor and blend for 3–4 minutes until smooth. Season to taste and pour into a jar or bowl, cover and chill until ready to use.

Makes 1 x 400 g (13 oz) jar

NUTRIENT ANALYSIS PER TABLESPOON SERVING 167 kJ – 40 kcal – 2 g protein – 3 g carbohydrate – 2 g sugars – 3 g fat – 1 g saturates – 0.4 g fibre – 14 mg sodium

FRESH TOMATO RELISH

Quick to prepare, and packed with summer flavours, this zesty, fresh relish resembles a salsa in its consistency. Serve it with almost anything from kebabs and rice dishes to breads.

INGREDIENTS 450 g (14½ oz) ripe plum tomatoes, deseeded and finely chopped │ ½ small red onion, finely diced │ 2 garlic cloves, finely diced │ 1 green chilli, deseeded if desired, sliced very thinly │ small handful of chopped coriander leaves │ juice of 2 limes │ salt

ONE Place the tomatoes, onion and garlic in a bowl. **TWO** Add the green chilli and coriander leaves to the tomato mixture. **THREE** Squeeze over the lime juice, season, cover and allow to sit at room temperature for 30 minutes before serving to allow the flavours to develop.

Serves 4

NUTRIENT ANALYSIS PER TABLESPOON SERVING 37 kJ – 9 kcal – 0 g protein – 2 g carbohydrate – 1 g sugars – 1 g fat – 0 g saturates – 0.5 g fibre – 4 mg sodium

HEALTHY TIP Every ingredient in this fresh, piquant relish is packed with goodness. Tomatoes are rich in the super-phytochemical lycopene; onions, chillies and garlic are great immunity-boosters; coriander contains useful flavonoids; and limes provide vitamin C.

SHALLOT THORAN

This wonderful, fresh thoran is a lightly cooked 'salad' or relish, that accompanies nearly every southern Indian meal to provide a crunchy contrast to the saucy 'wet' dishes.

INGREDIENTS 2 tablespoons light olive oil │ 1 teaspoon black mustard seeds │ 1 teaspoon urad dhal │ 8–10 curry leaves │ 250 g (8 oz) shallots, finely diced │ 1 red chilli, deseeded and finely diced │ 100 g (3½ oz) freshly grated coconut │ salt

ONE Heat the oil in a nonstick frying pan and when hot add the mustard seeds. As soon as they start to 'pop', add the urad dhal and stir-fry for 1–2 minutes, until the dhal turns a golden brown. **TWO** Add the curry leaves, shallots and green chilli and stir-fry over a medium heat for 5 minutes or until the shallots have softened slightly. Add the grated coconut, stir-fry for 1–2 minutes, then remove the pan from the heat. Season and serve.

Serves 4

NUTRIENT ANALYSIS PER TABLESPOON SERVING 707 kJ – 170 kcal – 2 g protein – 7 g carbohydrate – 5 g sugars – 15 g fat – 9 g saturates – 4 g fibre – 7 mg sodium

HEALTHY TIP Shallots belong to the same family as garlic. Some scientific studies have shown that the allium family increase the levels of good cholestrol in the body. This good cholestrol helps to carry the bad cholestrol away from the arteries in our bodies and so may help reduce the risk of heart disease.

recipe illustrated on pages 212–213

MANGO AND NIGELLA PICKLE

This pickle is really quick to prepare and makes a great addition to any rice and curry dish. Raw green mangoes are widely available from any good Asian greengrocer.

INGREDIENTS 500 g (1 lb) raw green mangoes, washed, stoned and cut into 1 cm (½ inch) pieces | 2 teaspoons coarse red chilli powder | 2 garlic cloves, finely chopped | 6 tablespoons golden caster sugar | 4 tablespoons white wine vinegar | 2 teaspoons nigella (black onion) seeds | 2 teaspoons sea salt

ONE Place all the ingredients in a small saucepan and cook over a medium heat for about 10 minutes. Remove from the heat, stir and allow to cool. **TWO** When cool, pour into a sterilized jar and cover. The pickle will keep for up to one week in the refrigerator.

Serves 4

NUTRIENT ANALYSIS PER SERVING 587 kJ – 138 kcal – 1.25 g protein – 33.5 g carbohydrate – 25.5 g sugars – 1 g fat – 0.25 g saturates – 0.25 g fibre – 1021.5 mg sodium

HEALTHY TIP Mangoes are excellent sources of vitamin C, carotenoids, fibre and potassium. Studies have shown that they have the ability to improve health and boost immunity.

DESSERTS A

ND DRINKS

MANGO, CARDAMOM AND CHILLI ICE

Beautifully flavoured, with a hidden 'kick' from the chilli powder, this ice made from the sweetest mangoes and gently spiced with crushed cardamom seeds, will have you wishing for more.

INGREDIENTS 5 large, ripe sweet mangoes, peeled, stoned and flesh removed, or 300 ml (½ pint) fresh mango purée | 1 teaspoon crushed cardamom seeds | ¼ teaspoon chilli powder | 200 ml (7 fl oz) light vanilla yogurt | wedges of fresh mango or fresh cherries, to serve (optional)

ONE Place the flesh of the mango in a food processor with the cardamom seeds, chilli powder and yogurt. **TWO** Blend until smooth, then tip the contents into an ice-cream maker and follow the manufacturer's instructions. If you don't have an ice-cream maker, place the contents in a freezer-proof container, cover and freeze for 2–3 hours. **THREE** Using a fork, break up the crystals that form towards the side of the container and stir to break up the mixture. Repeat this step four or five times (every 30 minutes or so) until the mixture is smooth and firm. Cover and freeze until ready to serve. **FOUR** Remove the ice cream from the freezer 10–15 minutes before serving and then scoop it into short dessert glasses or bowls and serve with wedges of fresh mango or fresh cherries if desired.

Serves 4

NUTRIENT ANALYSIS PER SERVING 660 kJ – 154 kcal – 3 g protein – 36 g carbohydrate – 35 g sugars – 1 g fat – 0 g saturates – 0 g fibre – 39 mg sodium

HEALTHY TIP Chillies are rich in carotenoids and vitamin C and are thought to help increase blood flow. They also have antibacterial properties which make them a favourite for beating colds and flu.

recipe illustrated on pages 222–223

MINTED MELON FRUIT SALAD WITH GINGER

Light and refreshing, this flavoursome fruit salad is the perfect way to end a meal and will help to cleanse the palate. The addition of ginger gives it a real bite and helps to enhance the delicate flavour of the melon.

INGREDIENTS 1 honeydew melon, about 300–400 g (10–13 oz) │ 1 charantais melon, about 300–400 g (10 13 oz) │ ½ small watermelon, about 300–400 g (10–13 oz) │ 1 cantaloupe melon, about 300–400 g (10–13 oz) │ 2 tablespoons finely chopped stem ginger │ 2 tablespoons syrup from the stem ginger │ 1 tablespoon lemon juice │ 3 tablespoons very finely chopped mint leaves

ONE Peel, deseed and cut the flesh of the melons into bite-sized cubes or, using a melon-baller, scoop out balls, reserving any juices from the fruit. Place the reserved fruit and any juices in a large serving bowl. **TWO** Sprinkle the stem ginger, syrup, lemon juice and mint leaves over the reserved fruit. Toss to mix well and if time permits, chill for 30 minutes before serving.

Serves 4

NUTRIENT ANALYSIS PER SERVING 1109 kJ – 259 kcal – 5 g protein – 60 g carbohydrate – 60 g sugars – 2 g fat – 0 g saturates – 7 g fibre – 207 mg sodium

HEALTHY TIP Melons are a natural diuretic and have a cleansing effect on the digestive system. Orange- and red-fleshed melons, such as cantaloupe and watermelon, also contain health-promoting betacarotene.

recipe illustrated on pages 226–227

WATERMELON, LIME, CHILLI AND VODKA GRANITAS

Icy cool, with a kick from the chilli and vodka, this unusual dessert has a slushy consistency and is perfect after a fiery meal.

INGREDIENTS ½ small watermelon, seeds discarded and cut into cubes │ 4 tablespoons caster sugar │ 1 teaspoon finely diced red chilli │ 100 ml (3½ fl oz) water │ juice and finely grated zest of 1 lime │ 3 tablespoons vodka

ONE Put the melon in a food processor and blend until smooth. **TWO** Place the sugar, chilli and the measured water in a small saucepan and bring to the boil, reduce the heat, add the lime juice and zest and gently simmer for 1 minute, stirring until all the sugar has dissolved. Remove from the heat and when cool add to the watermelon mixture with the vodka. Blend until smooth and then transfer the mixture to a wide freezer-proof container. Cover and freeze for 4–5 hours. **THREE** To serve, remove from the freezer and stir vigorously with a fork to break it up into a mass of small ice crystals. Alternatively, you can place the frozen mixture in the food processor and pulse briefly until you have a slushy consistency. Spoon the mixture into frozen glasses and serve immediately.

Serves 4

NUTRIENT ANALYSIS PER SERVING 563 kJ – 133 kcal – 1 g protein – 27 g carbohydrate – 27 g sugars – 1 g fat – 0 g saturates – 1 g fibre – 3 mg sodium

HEALTHY TIP Granitas, which are rather like a slushy sorbet, make a much healthier choice than ice cream. They're virtually fat-free and this version contains very little sugar, relying on the natural sweetness of the watermelon instead.

recipe illustrated on pages 230–231

SWEET VERMICELLI WITH SAFFRON

INGREDIENTS 2 tablespoons light olive oil | 125 g (4 oz) brown rice vermicelli | 750 ml (1¼ pints) semi-skimmed milk | large pinch of saffron threads | ½ teaspoon crushed cardamom seeds | 6 tablespoons golden caster sugar | 200 g (7 oz) raisins | 100 g (3½ oz) chopped mixed nuts, to serve

ONE Heat the oil in a heavy-based saucepan. Break the vermicelli into 4 cm (1½ inch) lengths and place it in the pan. Stir-fry over a gentle heat for 4–5 minutes until lightly golden, then pour in the milk and bring it to the boil. **TWO** Add the saffron, cardamom and sugar and cook while stirring over a medium heat for 15–20 minutes until thickened. Stir in the raisins and cook for 2–3 minutes, then remove from the heat. **THREE** Transfer the mixture into individual bowls, allow to cool and chill for 3–4 hours. Sprinkle over the nuts and serve immediately.

Serves 4

NUTRIENT ANALYSIS PER SERVING 2523 kJ – 600 kcal – 17 g protein – 91 g carbohydrate – 65 g sugars – 21 g fat – 5 g saturates – 5 g fibre – 140 mg sodium

PAPAYA AND POMEGRANATE FRUIT SALAD

INGREDIENTS 1 large ripe papaya or 2 smaller ones, deseeded and cut into bite-sized cubes │ 1 pomegranate │ 2 teaspoons clear honey │ juice of 1 lime │ ¼ teaspoon crushed black pepper │ 1 tablespoon ginger wine │ mint leaves, to decorate (optional)

ONE Place the prepared papaya in a large, shallow serving bowl. **TWO** Cut the pomegranate in half widthways and remove the seeds (the easiest way to do this is to tap the fruit with a heavy spoon and allow the seeds to drop off). Add to the papaya and mix well. **THREE** Put the honey, lime juice, pepper and ginger wine into a small bowl and stir to mix well. Drizzle this over the fruit and gently toss to mix well. Decorate with mint leaves before serving, if liked.

Serves 4

NUTRIENT ANALYSIS PER SERVING 423 kJ – 100 kcal – 1 g protein – 25 g carbohydrate – 4 g sugars – 0 g fat – 0 g saturates – 0 g fibre – 8 mg sodium

HEALTHY TIP Papayas are an excellent choice for dessert. They contain the enzyme papain, which is said to help the digestion of protein.

PISTACHIO AND SULTANA RICE PUDDING

Using ground rice for this pudding gives it a smooth, creamy texture that contrasts well with the plump, juicy sultanas and the bite of the pale green pistachio nuts.

INGREDIENTS 50 g (2 oz) coarsely ground rice │ ¼ teaspoon cardamom seeds, crushed │ 900 ml (1½ pints) semi-skimmed milk │ 6 tablespoons golden caster sugar │ 1 tablespoon rosewater │ 4 tablespoons chopped pistachio nuts │ 2 tablespoons golden sultanas

TO DECORATE pistachio nuts, sultanas

ONE Place the rice in a saucepan with the cardamom and 600 ml (1 pint) of the milk. Bring to the boil, stirring often. **TWO** Add the remaining milk and cook over a medium heat for 10–12 minutes or until the mixture thickens slightly. Stir in the sugar and rosewater and continue to cook for 2–3 minutes. **THREE** Stir in the pistachio nuts and sultanas and transfer the mixture into 4 individual bowls. Chill for 3–4 hours, then serve, decorated with chopped pistachio nuts and sultanas.

Serves 4

NUTRIENT ANALYSIS PER SERVING 1507 kJ – 357 kcal – 12 g protein – 53 g carbohydrate – 41 g sugars – 12 g fat – 2 g saturates – 1 g fibre – 127 mg sodium

HEALTHY TIP Rice pudding made with semi-skimmed milk is a healthy dessert choice. The sultanas are naturally sweet, so you don't need to add as much sugar as you would for a regular rice pudding.

recipe illustrated on pages 238–239

CARROT HALWA

This dessert has a fudge-like texture and delicious flavour and is usually made on special feast and festival days in India.

INGREDIENTS 1 litre (1¾ pints) semi-skimmed milk │ 375 g (12 oz) coarsely grated carrots │ 50 g (2 oz) unsalted butter │ 1 tablespoon golden syrup │ 100 g (3½ oz) golden caster sugar │ 150 g (5 oz) golden sultanas │ 4 cardamom pods, lightly crushed │ ½ teaspoon ground cinnamon │ low-fat yogurt or crème fraîche, to serve (optional)

ONE Place the milk, carrots, butter, golden syrup, caster sugar, sultanas, cardamom pods and cinnamon in a heavy-based saucepan. Bring to the boil then reduce the heat and cook gently for 20–25 minutes, stirring often. **TWO** Remove from the heat and serve warm or allow the mixture to cool and serve it chilled with a spoonful of low-fat yogurt or crème fraîche.

Serves 4

NUTRIENT ANALYSIS PER SERVING 1964 kJ – 465 kcal – 10 g protein – 79 g carbohydrate – 78 g sugars – 15 g fat – 9 g saturates – 5 g fibre – 200 mg sodium

HEALTHY TIP Carrots are known to have great blood-purifying qualities and are packed with vitamin D. They are even more nutritious cooked than raw. This is because the cell walls of raw carrots are tough and the cooking process helps break them down to make the betacarotene (the vegetable equivalent of vitamin A) easier for the body to absorb.

MASALA CHAI

This mildly spiced and soothing tea is drunk and served all over India, from little street stalls, to bustling stations and other public places. On trains, it is served in little clay cups, which adds to the flavour in a strange kind of way.

INGREDIENTS 2.5 cm (1 inch) piece of fresh root ginger, roughly chopped │ 6 cloves │ 2.5 cm (1 inch) piece of cassia bark or cinnamon stick │ 4 cardamom pods │ 500 ml (17 fl oz) water │ 200 ml (7 fl oz) semi-skimmed milk │ 3 tablespoons loose-leaf Indian tea (Darjeeling or Assam) │ 2 tablespoons golden caster sugar

ONE Place the ginger, cloves, cassia bark or cinnamon stick, cardamom, water, milk, tea and sugar in a heavy-based saucepan. **TWO** Bring the mixture to the boil, reduce the heat and allow it to cook gently for 2–3 minutes. **THREE** Remove it from the heat and strain the mixture, using a fine sieve. Pour it into cups or heatproof glasses and serve hot.

Serves 4

NUTRIENT ANALYSIS PER SERVING 959 kJ – 226 kcal – 8 g protein – 44 g carbohydrate – 42 g sugars – 3 g fat – 2 g saturates – 0 g fibre – 113 mg sodium

HEALTHY TIP The aromatic spices in this drink not only add flavour but also have healing properties. Ginger stimulates the circulation, while cardamom is said to help relieve nausea and indigestion and is also used to treat colds.

STRAWBERRY LASSI

Cool, creamy lassi is the classic drink enjoyed throughout India, where it is served either salty or sweet. This sweet version is made with strawberries and is absolutely delicious.

INGREDIENTS 400 g (13 oz) strawberries, roughly chopped │ 300 ml (½ pint) low-fat natural yogurt │ 30 g (1 oz) golden caster sugar │ 750 ml (1¼ pints) ice cold water │ a few drops of rosewater │ coarsely ground black pepper, to serve

ONE Place the strawberries in a food processor with half the iced water. Blend until smooth.
TWO Add the yogurt, sugar, remaining water and the rosewater and blend until smooth and frothy. Pour into chilled, tall glasses, sprinkle with black pepper and serve immediately.

Serves 4

NUTRIENT ANALYSIS PER SERVING 416 kJ – 99 kcal – 5 g protein – 20 g carbohydrate – 20 g sugars – 1 g fat – 0 g saturates – 2 g fibre – 68 mg sodium

HEALTHY TIP If you're in a hurry and haven't got time for a proper breakfast, this healthy, sustaining drink makes an excellent alternative.

CARROT, GINGER AND BEETROOT JUICE

It is essential to have a good fruit and vegetable juicer for this recipe, as it will extract all the nutrients from the ingredients in a smooth and silky manner. You can vary this juice by using 4–6 apples instead of the beetroot.

INGREDIENTS 10 large organic carrots │ 4 large beetroot │ 2.5 cm (1 inch) piece of fresh root ginger

ONE Put the vegetables through a juicer and extract all the juice. **TWO** Strain if desired and serve immediately.

Serves 4

NUTRIENT ANALYSIS PER SERVING 560 kJ – 133 kcal – 4 g protein – 29 g carbohydrate – 27 g sugars – 1 g fat – 0 g saturates – 1 g fibre – 155 mg sodium

HEALTHY TIP Beetroot is full of folic acid and manganese and carrot juice full of biotin, which helps to maintain hair, nerves and skin.

ALMOND MILK SHERBET

Also known as *thandai*, this cool, milky and soothing drink is usually drunk at religious festivals and on festal occasions such as *Holi* (the festival of spring) and *Divali* (the festival of lights).

INGREDIENTS 200 g (7 oz) ground almonds │ ½ teaspoon crushed cardamom seeds │ pinch of grated nutmeg │ 50 g (2 oz) golden caster sugar │ pinch of turmeric (optional) │ 1.5 litres (2½ pints) semi-skimmed milk

ONE Place all the ingredients in a heavy-based saucepan and bring to the boil. Remove from the heat and allow to infuse for 15–20 minutes. **TWO** Strain the mixture through a fine metal sieve and chill for 5–6 hours, or overnight. **THREE** To serve, fill 4 tall glasses with ice and pour over the almond sherbet.

Serves 4

NUTRIENT ANALYSIS PER SERVING 2215 kJ – 519 kcal – 23 g protein – 36 g carbohydrate – 34 g sugars – 34 g fat – 6 g saturates – 6 g fibre – 213 mg sodium

ICED CARDAMOM COFFEE

This aromatic, sweetly spiced coffee is delicious at any time of day – first thing in the morning, after lunch, mid-afternoon or even in the evening.

INGREDIENTS 5–6 cardamom pods, roughly crushed | 2.5 cm (1 inch) piece of cassia bark or cinnamon stick | 300 ml (½ pint) semi-skimmed milk | 300 ml (½ pint) good, strong black coffee, chilled | sugar, to taste (optional) | single cream or vanilla ice cream, to serve (optional)

ONE Place the cardamom pods in a heavy-based saucepan with the cassia or cinnamon and the milk. Bring to the boil, remove from the heat and allow to infuse until cooled. **TWO** Put the chilled coffee in a blender and strain the spiced milk into it. Blend until smooth, stir in sugar to taste, if using, and return the mixture to the refrigerator; chill for 2–3 hours. **THREE** To serve, pour the chilled coffee mixture into chilled, ice-filled glasses. Top the glasses with a small spoonful of single cream or a small scoop of vanilla ice cream.

Serves 4

NUTRIENT ANALYSIS PER SERVING 152 kJ – 36 kcal – 3 g protein – 4 g carbohydrate – 4 g sugars – 1 g fat – 1 g saturates – 0 g fibre – 42 mg sodium

HEALTHY TIP If you're watching your weight or keeping an eye on your fat intake, don't add the cream or ice cream to this coffee. It's just as good without.

MINT AND LEMON GRASS TEA

In India, a varied assortment of herbs and spices are added to hot water or milk to make a selection of teas that are considered detoxifying. This particular tea has a fresh, clean fragrance – perfect for cleansing the palate.

INGREDIENTS 750 ml (1¼ pints) water | 4 lemon grass stalks, lightly crushed to release the oils | small handful of mint leaves | 1 tablespoon honey (optional)

ONE Bring the water to the boil in a large saucepan. Add the lemon grass stalks and boil for 5–6 minutes; remove from the heat. **TWO** Add the mint leaves and honey, if using, cover and allow to infuse for 10 minutes. **THREE** Serve in cups or glasses. If preferred, this mixture can be served chilled, in a tall glass with plenty of ice.

Serves 4

NUTRIENT ANALYSIS PER SERVING 5 kJ – 1 kcal – 0 g protein – 0 g carbohydrate – 0 g sugars – 0 g fat – 0 g saturates – 0 g fibre – 0 mg sodium

HEALTHY TIP This calming tea stimulates digestion, so is perfect for serving to guests after a large meal.

ACKNOWLEDGEMENTS

EXECUTIVE EDITOR Nicky Hill

PROJECT EDITOR Charlotte Macey

DEPUTY CREATIVE DIRECTOR AND DESIGN Geoff Fennell

PHOTOGRAPHY Jason Lowe / © Octopus Publishing Group Ltd

SENIOR PRODUCTION CONTROLLER Martin Croshaw

FOOD STYLIST Sunil Vijayakar